3A

PRIMARY MATHEMATICS
Standards Edition

TEXTBOOK

Marshall Cavendish
Education

SM Singapore Math Inc®

Blank

Original edition published under the title Primary Mathematics Textbook 3A
© 1982 Curriculum Planning & Development Division, Ministry of Education, Singapore
Published by Times Media Private Limited

This edition © 2008 Marshall Cavendish International (Singapore) Private Limited

Published by Marshall Cavendish Education
An imprint of Marshall Cavendish International (Singapore) Private Limited
Times Centre, 1 New Industrial Road, Singapore 536196
Customer Service Hotline: (65) 6213 9444
E-mail: tmesales@sg.marshallcavendish.com
Website: www.marshallcavendish.com/education

Marshall Cavendish Corporation
99 White Plains Road
Tarrytown, NY 10591
U.S.A.
Tel: (1-914) 332 8888
Fax: (1-914) 332 8882
E-mail: mcc@marshallcavendish.com
Website: www.marshallcavendish.com

Distributed by
Singapore Math Inc
19535 SW 129th Avenue
Tualatin, OR 97062
U.S.A.
Website: www.singaporemath.com

First published 2008
Reprinted 2009 (twice), 2010 (twice), 2011 (twice), 2012, 2013, 2014

Primary Mathematics (Standards Edition) Textbook 3A
ISBN 978-0-7614-6980-3

Printed in Malaysia

Primary Mathematics (Standards Edition) is adapted from Primary Mathematics Textbook 3A (3rd Edition), originally developed by the
Ministry of Education, Singapore. This edition contains new content developed by Marshall Cavendish International (Singapore) Private
Limited, which is not attributable to the Ministry of Education, Singapore.

We would like to acknowledge the Project Team from the Ministry of Education, Singapore, that developed the original Singapore Edition:
Project Director: Dr Kho Tek Hong
Team Members: Hector Chee Kum Hoong, Chip Wai Lung, Liang Hin Hoon, Lim Eng Tann,
                Rosalind Lim Hui Cheng, Ng Hwee Wan, Ng Siew Lee
Curriculum Specialists: Christina Cheong Ngan Peng, Ho Juan Beng, Sin Kwai Meng

Our thanks to Richard Askey, Emeritus Professor of Mathematics (University of Wisconsin, Madison) and Madge Goldman, President
(Gabriella and Paul Rosenbaum Foundation), for their help and advice in the production of Primary Mathematics (Standards Edition).

We would also like to recognize the contributions of Jennifer Kempe (Curriculum Advisor, Singapore Math Inc) and Bill Jackson
(Math Coach, School No. 2, Paterson, New Jersey) to Primary Mathematics (Standards Edition).

PREFACE

PRIMARY MATHEMATICS (Standards Edition)
is a complete program from the publishers of
Singapore's successful *Primary Mathematics*
series. Newly adapted to align with the
Mathematics Framework for California Public
Schools, the program aims to equip students
with sound concept development, critical
thinking and efficient problem-solving skills.

Mathematical concepts are introduced in the
opening pages and taught to mastery through
specific learning tasks that allow for immediate
assessment and consolidation.

The **modeling method** enables
students to visualize and solve
mathematical problems quickly
and efficiently.

The **Concrete → Pictorial → Abstract**
approach enables students to encounter
math in a meaningful way and translate
mathematical skills from the concrete to
the abstract.

The **pencil icon** 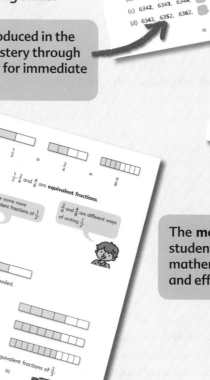 Exercise 18, pages 18-20 provides quick and easy
reference from the Textbook to the relevant Workbook pages.
The **direct correlation** of the Workbook to the Textbook
facilitates focused review and evaluation.

New mathematical concepts are introduced through a **spiral progression** that builds on concepts already taught and mastered.

1. A dog has four legs. How many legs do 7 dogs have?

Number of dogs	1	2	3	4	5	6	7
Number of legs	4	8	12	16	20	24	

$4 + 4 + 4 + 4 + 4 + 4 + 4 = $

$7 \times 4 = $

7 dogs have [ ] legs.

I can multiply the number of dogs by 4.

2. A toy car costs $5. How much do 8 toy cars cost?

Number of cars	1	2	3	4	5	6	7	8
Cost	$5	$10	$15	$20	$25	$30	$	$

The cost equals the number of cars multiplied by 5.

$8 \times 5 = $

8 toy cars cost $ [ ].

69

---

12. Find the product of 245 and 3.

Multiply the ones by 3.
$\begin{array}{r} 2\ 4\ 5 \\ \times\quad 3 \\ \hline \end{array}$

Multiply the tens by 3.
$\begin{array}{r} 2\ 4\ 5 \\ \times\quad 3 \\ \hline \end{array}$

Multiply the hundreds by 3.
$\begin{array}{r} 2\ 4\ 5 \\ \times\quad 3 \\ \hline \end{array}$

13. (a) Estimate the value of 212 × 4.

212 is 200 rounded to the nearest hundred.

$200 \times 4 = $

The value of 212 × 4 is about [ ].

(b) Find the value of 212 × 4.

$212 \times 4 = $

$\begin{array}{r} 2\ 1\ 2 \\ \times\quad 4 \\ \hline 8\ 4\ 8 \end{array}$

848 is close to 800. The answer is reasonable.

The value of 212 × 4 is [ ].

88

Metacognition is employed as a strategy for learners to monitor their thinking processes in problem solving. Speech and thought bubbles provide guidance through the thought processes, making even the most challenging problems accessible to students.

The color patch [ ] is used to invite active student participation and to facilitate lively discussion about the mathematical concepts taught.

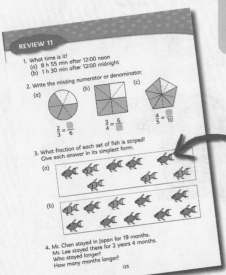

REVIEW 11

1. What time is it?
   (a) 8 h 55 min after 12:00 noon
   (b) 1 h 30 min after 12:00 midnight

2. Write the missing numerator or denominator.
   (a) $\frac{2}{3} = \frac{ }{6}$
   (b) $\frac{3}{4} = \frac{6}{ }$
   (c) $\frac{4}{5} = \frac{ }{10}$

3. What fraction of each set of fish is striped? Give each answer in its simplest form.
   (a)
   (b)

4. Mr. Chen stayed in Japan for 19 months. Mr. Lee stayed there for 2 years 4 months. Who stayed longer? How many months longer?

125

Regular **reviews** in the Textbook provide consolidation of concepts learned.

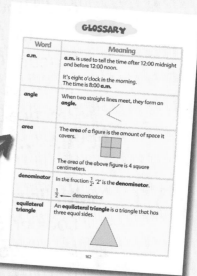

GLOSSARY

Word	Meaning
a.m.	**a.m.** is used to tell the time after 12:00 midnight and before 12:00 noon.
	It's eight o'clock in the morning. The time is 8:00 **a.m.**
angle	When two straight lines meet, they form an **angle**.
area	The **area** of a figure is the amount of space it covers.
	The area of the above figure is 4 square centimeters.
denominator	In the fraction $\frac{1}{2}$, '2' is the **denominator**. $\frac{1}{2}$ ← denominator
equilateral triangle	An **equilateral triangle** is a triangle that has three equal sides.

162

The **glossary** effectively combines pictorial representation with simple mathematical definitions to provide a comprehensive reference guide for students.

CONTENTS

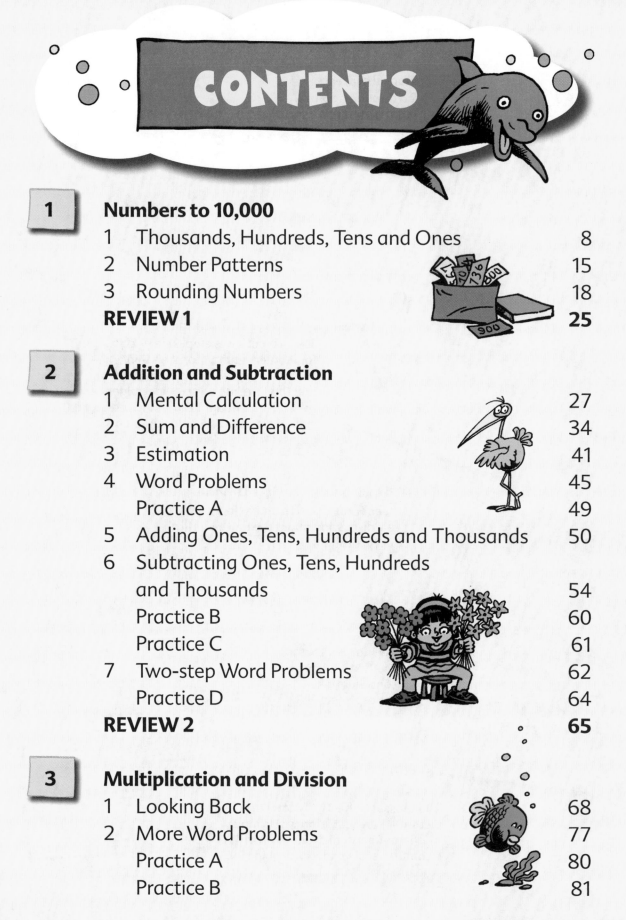

1 NUMBERS TO 10,000

1 Thousands, Hundreds, Tens and Ones

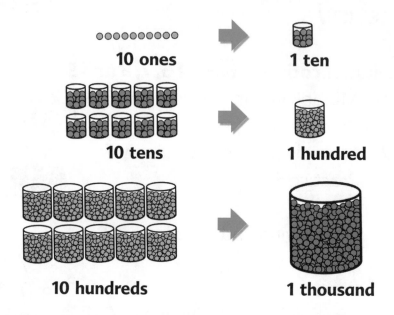

10 ones ➡ 1 ten

10 tens ➡ 1 hundred

10 hundreds ➡ 1 thousand

(a) Sam collected some marbles.

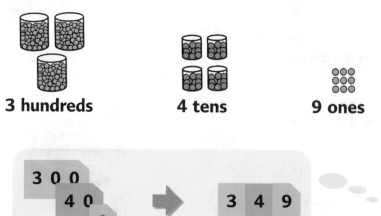

3 hundreds   4 tens   9 ones

| 3 0 0 |
| 4 0 |
| 9 | ➡ | 3 4 9 |

300 + 40 + 9 = ☐

(b) His sister also collected some marbles.

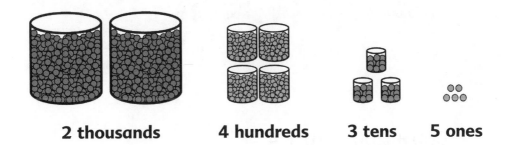

2 thousands   **4 hundreds**   **3 tens**   **5 ones**

$2000 + 400 + 30 + 5 = \boxed{}$

How many marbles did she collect?

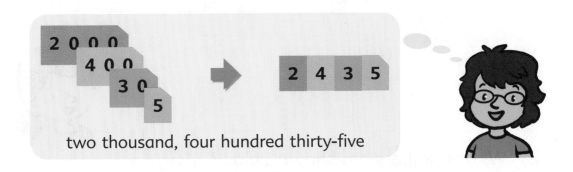

two thousand, four hundred thirty-five

$2000 + 400 + 30 + 5$ is the **expanded form** of 2435.

2435 is the **standard form** of 2435.

(c) Read the numbers 5998 and 6012.

(d) Count from 5998 to 6012.

5998, 5999, 6000, ..., 6012

(e) Count from 9987 to 10,000.

1. Count the thousands, hundreds, tens and ones in this chart.

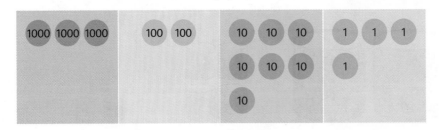

$$3000 + 200 + 70 + 4 = \boxed{}$$

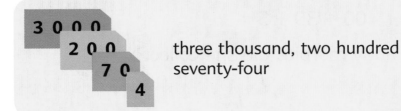

three thousand, two hundred seventy-four

2. What numbers are shown below?
   Read each number.
   Write each number in standard form and in words.

(a)

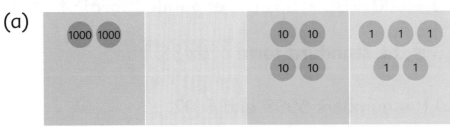

(b)

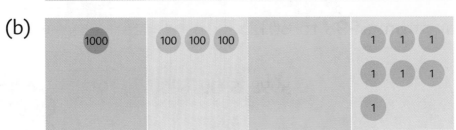

(c)

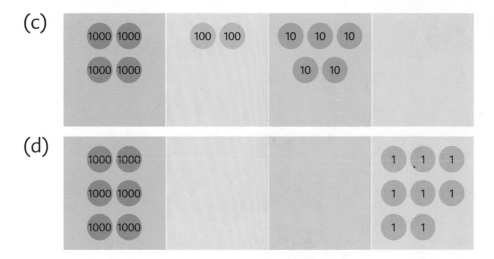

(d)

3. Write the numbers in standard form.
   (a) two thousand, one hundred sixty-three
   (b) eight thousand, eight
   (c) five thousand, three hundred
   (d) six thousand, forty

Exercise 1, pages 7-9

4. Write the numbers in expanded form.
   (a) 2578

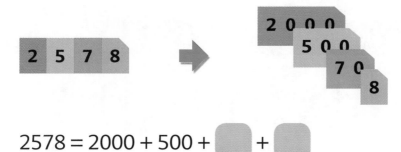

   $2578 = 2000 + 500 + \boxed{} + \boxed{}$

   (b) 7619
   (c) 4300

5.

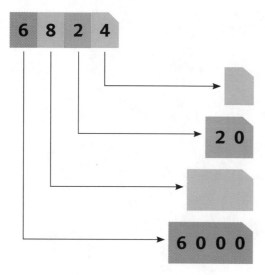

6824 is a 4-digit number.
The digit 2 stands for 20.
The digit 6 stands for 6000.
What does the digit 8 stand for?
What does the digit 4 stand for?

6. What does the digit **5** stand for in each of the following numbers?

(a) 3**5**21   (b) **5**213   (c) 12**5**3

7.

Thousands	Hundreds	Tens	Ones
3	4	6	8

In 3468, the digit 8 is in the **ones place**. Its **value** is 8.

The digit 6 is in the **tens place**. Its value is 60.

The digit [ ] is in the **hundreds place**. Its value is [ ].

The digit [ ] is in the **thousands place**. Its value is [ ].

8. What is the value of each digit in 8137?

Exercise 2, pages 10-11

9. Which is greater, 316 or 264?

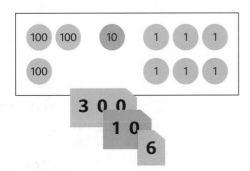 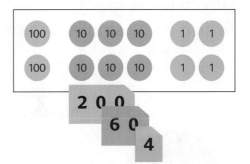

316 is greater than 264.

Compare the hundreds.
300 is greater than 200.
So, 316 > 264.

Which is smaller, 325 or 352?

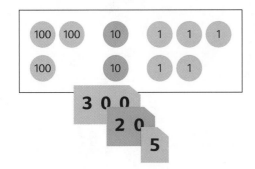 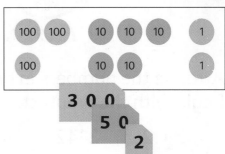

325 is less than 352.

When the hundreds are the
same, compare the tens.
20 < 50
So, 325 < 352.

(a) Which is greater, 4316 or 4264?
    Which is greater, 4316 or 5264?
(b) Which is smaller, 2325 or 2352?
    Which is smaller, 3325 or 2352?

10. Write >, < or = in place of each .

(a) 7031 ⬤ 7301   (b) 8004 ⬤ 8040

(c) 3756 ⬤ 3576   (d) 5698 ⬤ 5698

11. 5073,   4982,   4973
    Which is the greatest number?
    Which is the smallest number?

12.

100 is the smallest
3-digit number.

999 is the greatest
3-digit number.

What is the smallest 4-digit number?
What is the greatest 4-digit number?

13. Arrange the numbers in order.
    Begin with the greatest.

        3412,   3142,   4123,   2431

14. Arrange the numbers in order.
    Begin with the smallest.

        1892,   9003,   913,   1703

15. Use all the digits 0, 4 and 5 to
    make different 3-digit numbers.
    Which is the greatest number?
    Which is the smallest number?

    Do not begin a
    number with 0.

16. (a) What is the greatest 4-digit number that you can make
         using all the digits 0, 7, 2 and 8?

    (b) What is the smallest 4-digit number that you can make
         using all the digits 3, 7, 4 and 9?

Exercise 3, pages 12-13

② Number Patterns

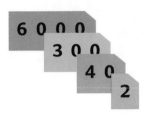

6 **3** 4 2

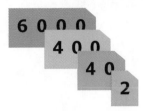

6 **4** 4 2

Which is more? How many more?

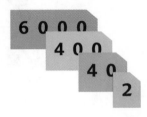

6 **4** 4 2

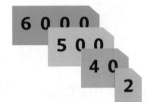

6 **5** 4 2

Which is more? How many more?

What number is 100 more than 6442?

What number is 100 more than 6542?

Complete the following regular number patterns.

(a) 6**3**42, 6**4**42, 6**5**42, ▢, ▢

(b) **6**342, **7**342, **8**342, ▢, ▢

(c) 634**2**, 634**3**, 634**4**, ▢, ▢

(d) 63**4**2, 63**5**2, 63**6**2, ▢, ▢

6342 $\xrightarrow{+100}$ 6442

6442 $\xrightarrow{+100}$ 6542

6542 $\xrightarrow{+?}$?

1. (a) What number is 100 more than 3624?

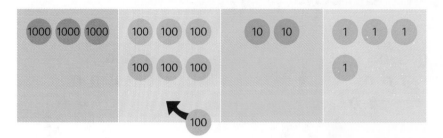

Add 1 hundred to 3624.

$3624 \xrightarrow{+100}$ ▢

(b) What number is 1 more than 3624?

(c) What number is 10 more than 3624?

(d) What number is 1000 more than 3624?

2. (a) What number is 1000 less than 5732?

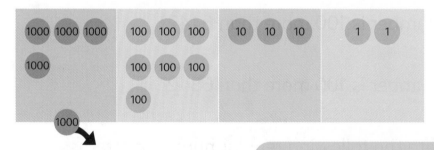

Subtract 1 thousand from 5732.

$5732 \xrightarrow{-1000}$ ▢

(b) What number is 1 less than 5732?

(c) What number is 10 less than 5732?

(d) What number is 100 less than 5732?

3. (a) Count by 10's from 1678 to 1728.
1678,   1688,   1698,   ...,   1728

(b) Count by 100's from 1678 to 2178.
1678,   1778,   1878,   ...,   2178

(c) Count by 1000's from 1678 to 8678.
1678,   2678,   3678,   ...,   8678

4. Complete the following regular number patterns.

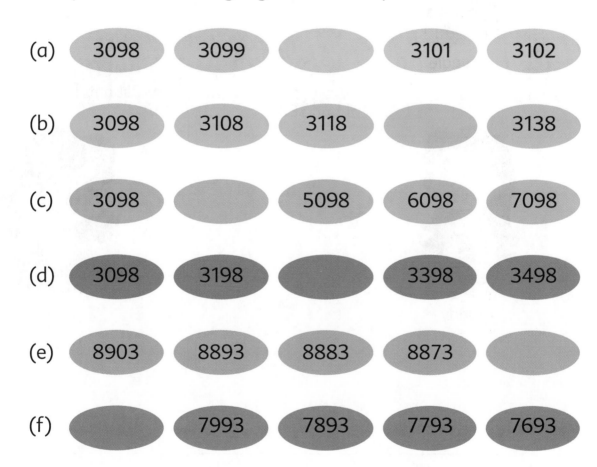

(a) 3098   3099   ⬭   3101   3102

(b) 3098   3108   3118   ⬭   3138

(c) 3098   ⬭   5098   6098   7098

(d) 3098   3198   ⬭   3398   3498

(e) 8903   8893   8883   8873   ⬭

(f) ⬭   7993   7893   7793   7693

Exercise 4, pages 14-16

3 Rounding Numbers

They **round** each of the numbers 61, 68 and 75 to
the nearest ten.

61 is between 60 and 70.
It is nearer to 60 than to 70.
So the nearest ten is 60.

61 is 60 when rounded to the nearest ten.

68 is between 60 and 70.
It is nearer to 70 than to 60.
So the nearest ten is 70.

68 is 70 when rounded to the nearest ten.

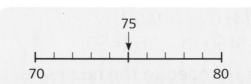

75 is halfway between 70 and 80.
We take 80 to be the nearest ten.

75 is 80 when rounded to the nearest ten.

1. Round each number to the nearest ten.
   (a) 29   (b) 38   (c) 82   (d) 95

2. Round each number to the nearest ten.
   (a) 234

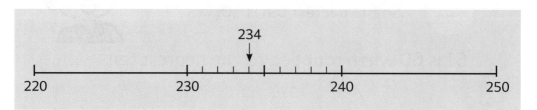

   234 is between 230 and 240.
   234 is nearer to 230 than to 240.

   234 is ⬜ when rounded to the nearest ten.

   (b) 1458

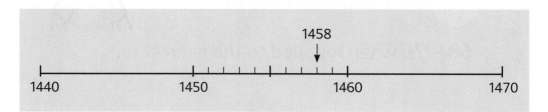

   1458 is between 1450 and 1460.
   1458 is nearer to 1460 than to 1450.

   1458 is ⬜ when rounded to the nearest ten.

   (c) 2735

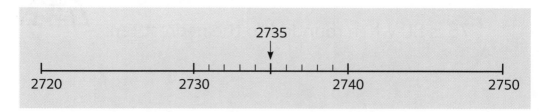

   2735 is halfway between 2730 and 2740.

   2735 is ⬜ when rounded to the nearest ten.

3. Round each number to the nearest ten.
   (a) 129   (b) 201   (c) 452   (d) 685

   (e) 2069   (f) 4355   (g) 4805   (h) 5508

 Exercise 5, pages 17-18

4. There are 2478 students in Lakeview School.
   (a) Round the number of students to the nearest ten.

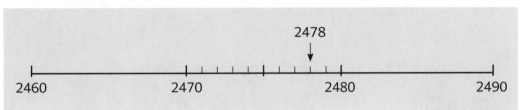

2478 is more than halfway between 2470 and 2480.
It is nearer to 2480 than to 2470.

2478 is ⬜ when rounded to the nearest ten.

   (b) Round the number of students to the nearest hundred.

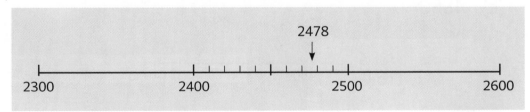

2478 is more than halfway between 2400 and 2500.
It is nearer to 2500 than to 2400.

2478 is ⬜ when rounded to the nearest hundred.

5. Mr. Ricci sold his car for $9125.
   Round this amount to the nearest $100.

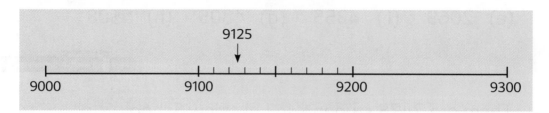

$9125 is $ [ ] when rounded to the nearest $100.

6. Round each number to the nearest hundred.

   (a) 345

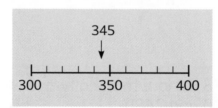

   (b) 3670

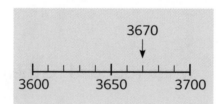

   (c) 4850

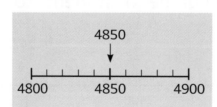

7. Round each number to the nearest hundred.
   (a) 320   (b) 486   (c) 650   (d) 980
   (e) 2915   (f) 3075   (g) 4308   (h) 5150
   (i) 9234   (j) 8520   (k) 7450   (l) 9990

Exercise 6, pages 19-20

8. There were 7355 people at a football game.

   (a) Round 7355 to the nearest ten.

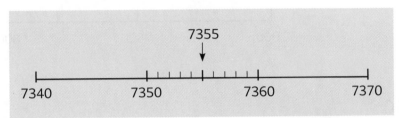

   7355 is halfway between 7350 and 7360.

   7355 is [ ] when rounded to the nearest ten.

   (b) Round 7355 to the nearest hundred.

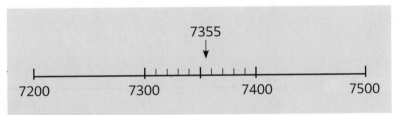

   7355 is [ ] when rounded to the nearest hundred.

   (c) Round 7355 to the nearest thousand.

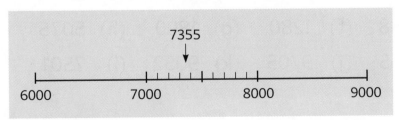

   7355 is [ ] when rounded to the nearest thousand.

9. Round to the nearest thousand.

(a) 4800

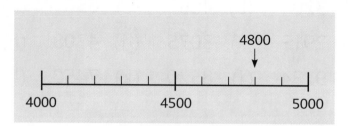

(b) 7455

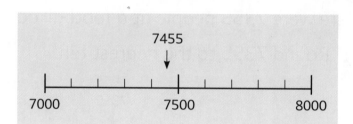

(c) 3010

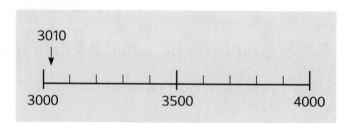

(d) 9580

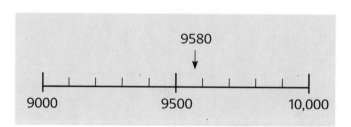

10. Round each number to the nearest thousand.

(a) 2680   (b) 8980   (c) 6499   (d) 3508

(e) 3058   (f) 1280   (g) 1800   (h) 5075

(i) 8765   (j) 9705   (k) 9052   (l) 7501

Exercise 7, pages 21-22

1. Write three thousand, six hundred in standard form.

2. Write 1347 in words.

3. Write 6352 in thousands, hundreds, tens and ones.

4. What number is shown in each of the following?

   (a) 1000 100 100 1 1 1 1 1

   (b) 1000 1000 1000 10 10

   (c) 1000 1000 10 10 10 1 1

5. Write the numbers in expanded form.
   (a) 1736

   (b) 7504

6. Which of the following is equal to 679?
   (a) 600 + 700 + 900   (b) 6 + 70 + 900

   (c) 600 + 70 + 9   (d) 6 + 7 + 9

7. Write > or < in place of each ⬤.

   (a) 7865 ⬤ 8567

   (b) 4104 ⬤ 4049

8. Which is the greatest number in the following?
   7171,   7711,   7117

9. Arrange these numbers in order.
   Begin with the smallest.

3500   3050   5003   350   3005

10. What is the value of the digit **8** in each of the following?
    (a) 7**8**92   (b) 346**8**   (c) **8**005   (d) 70**8**1

11. What does each digit in 5629 stand for?

12. Write the next three numbers for the following
    number pattern.

    2007,   2008,   2009,   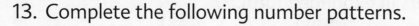 ,   ,

13. Complete the following number patterns.

    (a) 997,   998,   999,

    (b) 2080,   ,   2100,   2110

14. Round each number to the nearest ten.

    (a) 93   (b) 302   (c) 915   (d) 3487

15. Round 6497 to the nearest
    (a) hundred
    (b) thousand

2 ADDITION AND SUBTRACTION

1 Mental Calculation

Add 38 and 5.

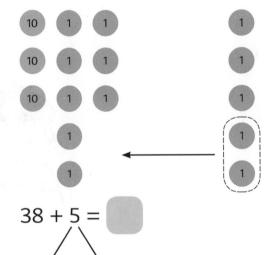

$$38 + 5 = \boxed{}$$

2   3

Make a 10 first.
38 + 5

2   3

38 + 2 = 40
40 + 3 = 43

---

1. Add.

   (a) 42 + 3

   2 + 3 < 10

   I can add the ones.
   42 + 3

   40   2

   2 + 3 = 5
   40 + 5 = 45

   $$42 + 3 = \boxed{}$$

   (b) 59 + 8   (c) 41 + 9

2. Add 46 and 27.

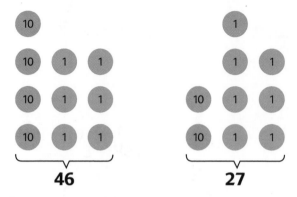

46 + 27
20   7
Add 20 to 46 first.

$46 \xrightarrow{+20} 66 \xrightarrow{+7} 73$

$46 + 27 = \boxed{}$

3. (a) $23 \xrightarrow{+10} \boxed{} \xrightarrow{+4} \boxed{}$

$23 + 14 = \boxed{}$

(b) $54 \xrightarrow{+30} \boxed{} \xrightarrow{+6} \boxed{}$

$54 + 36 = \boxed{}$

(c) $38 \xrightarrow{+40} \boxed{} \xrightarrow{+5} \boxed{}$

$38 + 45 = \boxed{}$

4. (a) What number is 3 more than 68?
   (b) What number is 20 more than 94?

5. Add.
   (a) 43 + 30   (b) 67 + 20   (c) 85 + 50
   (d) 72 + 5   (e) 33 + 7   (f) 64 + 8
   (g) 36 + 23   (h) 27 + 35   (i) 55 + 26

6. Add 58 and 16.

   58 + 16 = ⬜

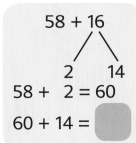

58 + 16

2   14

58 + 2 = 60

60 + 14 = ⬜

7. Add.
   (a) 39 + 8   (b) 58 + 34   (c) 45 + 65
   (d) 78 + 14   (e) 39 + 27   (f) 53 + 18

8. Add.
   (a) 26 + 49

   49 is 1 less than 50.

   $26 \xrightarrow{+50} 76 \xrightarrow{-1} 75$

   26 + 49 = ⬜

   (b) 35 + 49   (c) 48 + 17

9. Subtract 4 from 30.

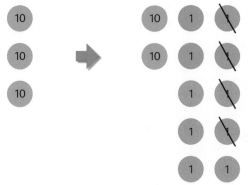

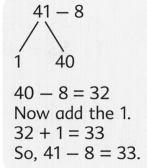

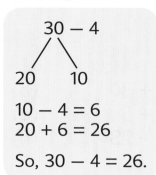

$30 - 4$

20   10

$10 - 4 = 6$
$20 + 6 = 26$

So, $30 - 4 = 26$.

$30 - 4 = $ ⬜

10. Subtract.

(a) $41 - 8$

$41 - 8$

1   40

$40 - 8 = 32$
Now add the 1.
$32 + 1 = 33$
So, $41 - 8 = 33$.

We can also subtract in
this way.
$41 - 8$
If I take away 1, I have
to take away 7 more.
$41 - 1 = 40$
$40 - 7 = 33$
So, $41 - 8 = 33$.

$41 - 8 = $ ⬜

(b) $60 - 5$ (c) $32 - 6$ (d) $87 - 9$

11. Subtract 34 from 87.

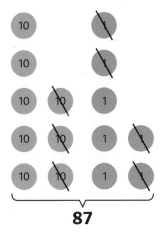

87 − 34

30   4

Subtract 30 from 87 first.

$$87 \xrightarrow{-30} 57 \xrightarrow{-4} 53$$

$$87 - 34 = \boxed{}$$

12. (a) $65 \xrightarrow{-10} \boxed{} \xrightarrow{-2} \boxed{}$

$$65 - 12 = \boxed{}$$

(b) $76 \xrightarrow{-40} \boxed{} \xrightarrow{-6} \boxed{}$

$$76 - 46 = \boxed{}$$

(c) $63 \xrightarrow{-20} \boxed{} \xrightarrow{-8} \boxed{}$

$$63 - 28 = \boxed{}$$

13. (a) What number is 2 less than 51?
    (b) What number is 30 less than 76?

14. Subtract.
    (a) 70 − 30   (b) 95 − 70
    (c) 68 − 60   (d) 58 − 6
    (e) 83 − 3   (f) 47 − 9

15. Subtract.
    (a) 48 − 32   (b) 56 − 24
    (c) 87 − 47   (d) 64 − 34
    (e) 85 − 59   (f) 63 − 55

16. Subtract.

    (a) 86 − 49

         86 − 49 = ⬜

    49 is 1 less than 50.

    86 $\xrightarrow{\ -\,50\ }$ 36 $\xrightarrow{\ +\,1\ }$ 37

    (b) 73 − 49   (c) 92 − 48

17. Subtract 18 from 90.

    90 − 18 = ⬜

    90 − 18
      / \
    70   20

    20 − 18 = 2
    90 − 18 = 70 + 2

18. Subtract.
    (a) 30 − 28   (b) 60 − 56
    (c) 70 − 65   (d) 50 − 17
    (e) 40 − 29   (f) 80 − 58
    (g) 40 − 16   (h) 70 − 47
    (i) 90 − 39   (j) 50 − 38

Exercise 2, pages 28-29

19. Solve.
  (a) 400 + 300
  (b) 424 + 300
  (c)   8 + 5
  (d)   80 + 50
  (e)   30 + 90
  (f) 430 + 90
  (g) 600 − 200
  (h) 629 − 200
  (i)   14 − 7
  (j) 140 − 70
  (k)   32 − 8
  (l) 320 − 80

20. (a) Add 483 and 98.

98 is 2 less than 100.

$$483 \xrightarrow{+100} 583 \xrightarrow{-2} 581$$

  483 + 98 = ◻

  (b) Subtract 98 from 483.

$$483 \xrightarrow{-100} 383 \xrightarrow{+2} 385$$

  483 − 98 = ◻

21. Find the value of
  (a)   48 + 99
  (b) 348 + 99
  (c) 560 + 95
  (d) 167 − 97
  (e) 992 − 97
  (f) 650 − 95

22. Add 13, 56, 38 and 74.

```
    2
    1 3          1 3
    5 6          5 6
    3 8          3 8
 +  7 4       +  7 4
 ──────       ──────
      1
```

Add 6 and 4 first: 6 + 4 = 10
Then add 8 and 3: 8 + 3 = 11
So, the total of the ones is
    10 + 11 = 21

This way of grouping the
ones and adding is easier
than adding in the order it
appears like this:
3 + 6 = 9, 9 + 8 = 17,
17 + 4 = 21

23. Find the value of 45 + 32 + 38 + 77.

33

 Exercise 3, pages 30-31

2 Sum and Difference

(a) What is the sum of 4 and 7?

To find the **sum**, we add the two numbers.

$$4 + 7 = \boxed{}$$

The sum of 4 and 7 is .

(b) What is the difference between 4 and 7?

To find the **difference**, we subtract the smaller number from the bigger number.

$$7 - 4 = \boxed{}$$

The difference between 4 and 7 is .

1.

(a) 8 + 5 = ☐

The sum of 8 and 5 is ☐.

(b) 8 − 5 = ☐

The difference between 8 and 5 is ☐.

2.

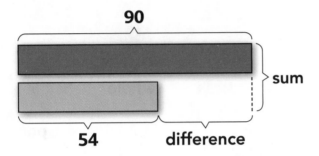

(a) The sum of 90 and 54 is ☐.

(b) The difference between 90 and 54 is ☐.

3. (a) The sum of 12 and 9 is ☐.

(b) The sum of two numbers is 21.
If one number is 9, the other number is ☐.

(c) The difference between 21 and 9 is ☐.

(d) The difference between 21 and 12 is ☐.

Exercise 4, pages 32-33

4. 40 + 25 =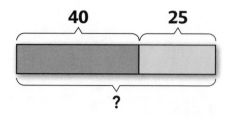

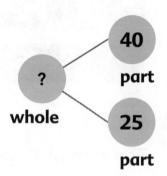

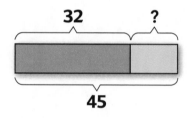

To find the whole, we add.

5. 32 + 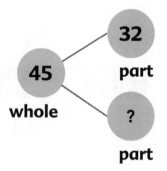 = 45

To find a part, we subtract.

45 − 32 =

6. 85 − 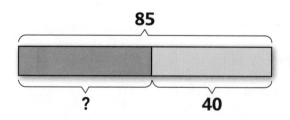 = 40

To find a part, we subtract.

85 − 40 =

7. 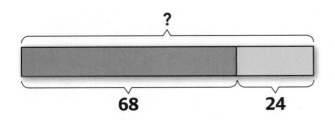 $- 24 = 68$

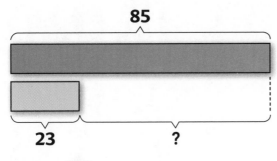

To find the whole, we add.

$68 + 24 = $ ▢

8. (a) $76 + $ ▢ $= 84$ (b) $72 - $ ▢ $= 66$

   (c) $84 - $ ▢ $= 69$ (d) ▢ $+ 34 = 87$

   (e) ▢ $- 22 = 60$ (f) ▢ $- 41 = 27$

   (g) $80 - $ ▢ $= 30 + 20$ (h) $15 + $ ▢ $= 20 - 1$

Exercise 5, pages 34-35

9. Compare 85 and 23.

We need to find the difference between 85 and 23.

85 is ▢ more than 23.

$85 = 23 + $ ▢

$85 - 23 = $ ▢

37

10. Compare 90 and 62.

   62 is  less than 90.

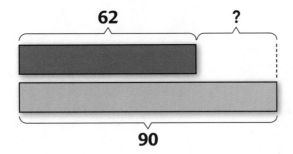

$$62 = 90 - \boxed{}$$

$$90 - 62 = \boxed{}$$

11. 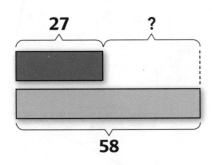 more than 27 is 58.

$$27 + \boxed{} = 58$$

$$58 - 27 = \boxed{}$$

12. What is 24 more than 21?

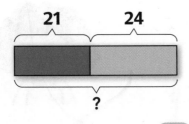

$$21 + 24 = \boxed{}$$

13. 29 is 14 less than 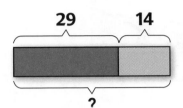.

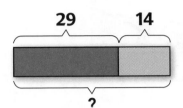

$$29 = \boxed{} - 14$$

$$29 + 14 = \boxed{}$$

14. Draw models to solve the following.

(a) 9 more than 49 is ⬜.

(b) 12 more than ⬜ is 45.

(c) ⬜ more than 62 is 99.

(d) 20 less than ⬜ is 36.

(e) ⬜ less than 90 is 55.

Exercise 6, pages 36-37

15. Sum or difference?

(a) 25 ⬤ 61 = 86

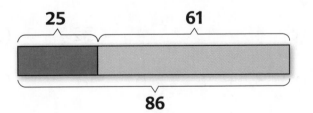

(b) 99 ⬤ 42 = 57

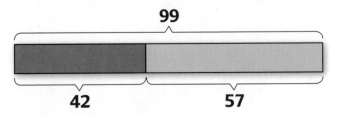

16. Write >, <, or = in place of each .

(a) 6 + 1 ◯ 6 + 3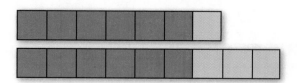

(b) 14 + 5 ◯ 14 + 8

(c) 23 + 81 ◯ 38 + 81

17. Write >, <, or = in place of each ◯.

(a) 10 − 5 ◯ 10 − 6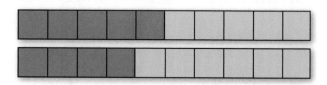

(b) 12 − 7 ◯ 12 − 3

(c) 86 − 15 ◯ 86 − 17

18. Find each sum or difference.
Then use >, <, or = in place of each ◯.

(a) 23 + 5 ◯ 23 − 5   (b) 82 + 10 ◯ 92 − 10

(c) 45 − 12 ◯ 45 − 32   (d) 14 + 26 ◯ 43 + 9

(e) 32 + 48 ◯ 61 − 18   (f) 36 + 47 ◯ 36 + 29

(g) 87 + 6 ◯ 28 − 14   (h) 62 + 21 ◯ 72 + 11

Exercise 7, pages 38-39

③ Estimation

(a) Estimate, then find the sum of 218 and 625.

$$\begin{array}{r} 2\,1\,8 \\ +\ \ 6\,2\,5 \\ \hline \end{array}$$

218 is about 200.
625 is about 600.

200 + 600 = 800

The answer should be about 800.

Add the ones.

$$\begin{array}{r} \overset{1}{2}\,1\,8 \\ +\ \ 6\,2\,5 \\ \hline 3 \end{array}$$

Add the tens.

$$\begin{array}{r} \overset{1}{2}\,1\,8 \\ +\ \ 6\,2\,5 \\ \hline 4\,3 \end{array}$$

Add the hundreds.

$$\begin{array}{r} \overset{1}{2}\,1\,8 \\ +\ \ 6\,2\,5 \\ \hline 8\,4\,3 \end{array}$$

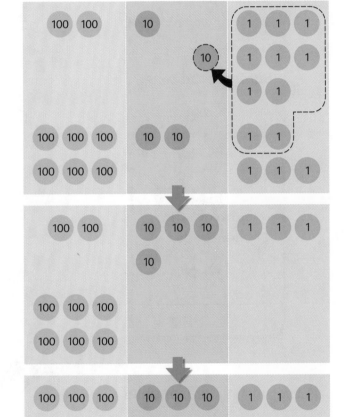

Is the answer reasonable?

843 is close to the estimated answer of 800.

The answer is reasonable.

(b) Estimate, then find the difference between 453 and 267.

$$\begin{array}{r} 4\;5\;3 \\ -\;2\;6\;7 \\ \hline \end{array}$$

453 is about 500.
267 is about 300.

$500 - 300 = 200$

The answer is reasonable if it is about 200.

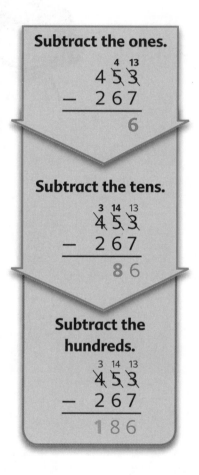

Subtract the ones.

$$\begin{array}{r} {}^{4}\;{}^{13}\;\\ 4\;\cancel{5}\;\cancel{3} \\ -\;2\;6\;7 \\ \hline 6 \end{array}$$

Subtract the tens.

$$\begin{array}{r} {}^{3}\;{}^{14}\;{}^{13}\\ \cancel{4}\;\cancel{5}\;\cancel{3} \\ -\;2\;6\;7 \\ \hline 8\;6 \end{array}$$

Subtract the hundreds.

$$\begin{array}{r} {}^{3}\;{}^{14}\;{}^{13}\\ \cancel{4}\;\cancel{5}\;\cancel{3} \\ -\;2\;6\;7 \\ \hline 1\;8\;6 \end{array}$$

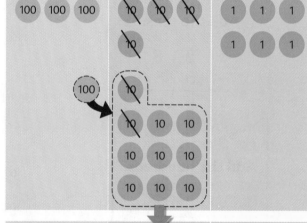

Is the answer reasonable?

We can also check our answer with addition.

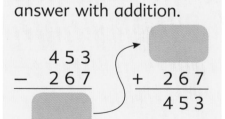

$$\begin{array}{r} 4\;5\;3 \\ -\;2\;6\;7 \\ \hline \end{array} \qquad \begin{array}{r} +\;2\;6\;7 \\ \hline 4\;5\;3 \end{array}$$

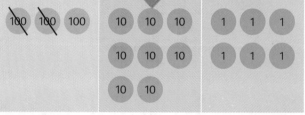

1. Estimate the value of 89 + 48 by rounding each number to the nearest ten.

89 is about 90.
48 is about 50.

$$90 + 50 = \boxed{}$$

The value of 89 + 48 is about 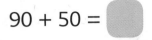.

2. Estimate the value of 336 + 568 by rounding each number to the nearest hundred.

336 is about 300.
568 is about 600.

$$300 + 600 = \boxed{}$$

The value of 336 + 568 is about 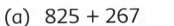.

3. Find the value of each of the following.
   Use estimation to see if your answers are reasonable.

   (a) 825 + 267   (b) 374 + 481   (c) 484 + 166
   (d) 906 − 524   (e) 695 − 167   (f) 800 − 325

4. Estimate, then find the value of 962 − 594.

962 − 594 is about .

962 − 594 is exactly .

I can check my answer by adding.

```
  9 6 2          +  5 9 4
−  5 9 4            9 6 2
```

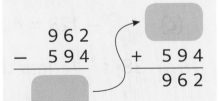

5. (a) Estimate the value of 469 − 52.

469 is about 500.
52 is about 50.

500 − 50 = 450

469 is about 470.
52 is about 50.

470 − 50 = 420

(b) Find the actual value of 469 − 52.

$$\begin{array}{r} 4\ 6\ 9 \\ -\ \ \ 5\ 2 \\ \hline \end{array}$$

469 − 52 =

(c) Which estimate was closer, 450 or 420?

6. Estimate, then find the value of
   (a) 435 + 48   (b) 282 + 27   (c) 955 + 87
   (d) 362 − 48   (e) 123 − 58   (f) 304 − 76

7. Find the missing numbers.
   Use estimation to see if your answers are reasonable.

   (a) ☐ + 406 = 592

   (b) 592 − ☐ = 421

   (c) ☐ − 123 = 402

   (d) 38 is ☐ less than 342.

   (e) ☐ more than 183 is 304.

   (f) 78 more than ☐ is 200.

44

Exercise 8, pages 40-41

4 Word Problems

Mary made 686 paper flowers. She sold some of them.
If 298 were left over, how many flowers did she sell?

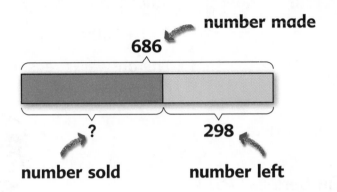

number made

686

? — number sold

298 — number left

To find the shaded part, we subtract the other part from the whole.

$686 - 298 = $

She sold ▢ flowers.

134 girls and 119 boys took part in an art competition.
How many more girls than boys were there?

$134 - 119 = $

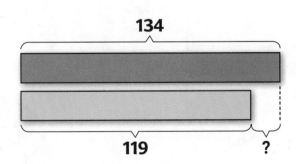

134

119   ?

There were ▢ more girls than boys.

1. A man sold 230 balloons at a carnival in the morning.
   He sold another 86 balloons in the evening.
   How many balloons did he sell in all?

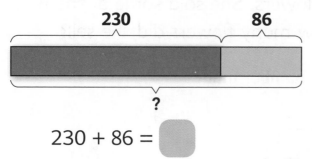

230 + 86 = ⬜

230 is about 200.
86 is about 100.

200 + 100 = 300

The answer is reasonable
if it is near 300.

He sold ⬜ balloons in all.

2. The sum of two numbers is 175.
   If one number is 49, what is the other number?

49 + ⬜ = 175

175 − ⬜ = ⬜

The other number is ⬜.

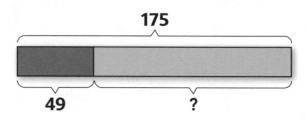

3. Lynn saved $184.
   She saved $63 more than Betty.
   How much did Betty save?

184 − 63 = ⬜

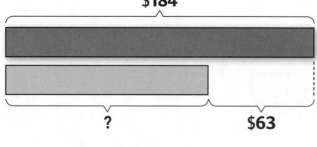

Betty saved $⬜.

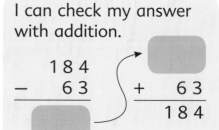

I can check my answer
with addition.

```
   1 8 4          ⬜
 −   6 3    +    6 3
   _____        _____
     ⬜          1 8 4
```

46

Exercise 9, pages 42-44

4. John read 32 pages in the morning.
   He read 14 fewer pages in the afternoon.

   (a) How many pages did he read in the afternoon?
   (b) How many pages did he read altogether?

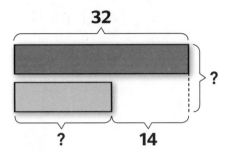

   (a) 32 − 14 = 18
       He read 18 pages in the afternoon.

   (b) 32 + 18 = 50
       He read 50 pages altogether.

5. The difference between two numbers is 68.

   (a) If the smaller number is 153, what is the
       greater number?

   (b) What is the sum of the two numbers?

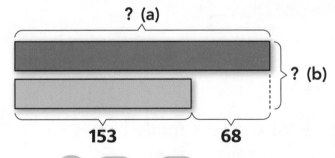

   (a) 153 ◯ ▢ = ▢
       The greater number is ▢.

   (b) 153 ◯ ▢ = ▢
       The sum of the two numbers is ▢.

I can use the answer
from part (a) to solve
part (b).

6. This table shows the number of crackers made by three machines in one hour.

(a) What is the total number of crackers made by Machine A and Machine B?

Machine A	468
Machine B	652
Machine C	945

468   652

?

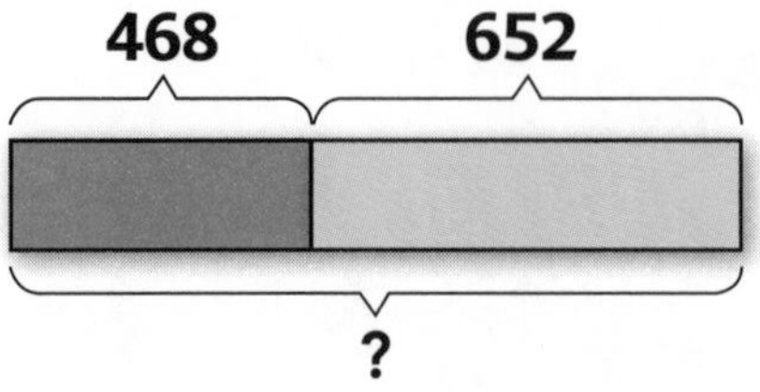

468 + 652 = ⬜

The total number of crackers made by Machine A and Machine B is ⬜.

(b) What is the total number of crackers made by the three machines?

⬜   945

?

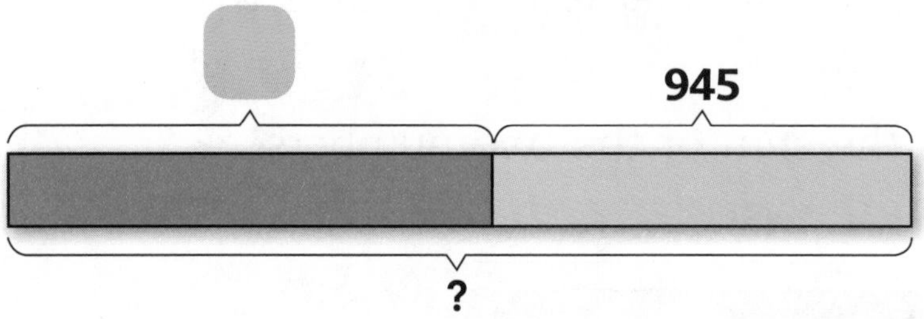

⬜ + 945 = ⬜

The total number of crackers made by the three machines is ⬜.

Exercise 10, pages 45-47

1. Leela has 254 rubber bands.
   Her friend gives her 58 more.
   How many rubber bands does she have now?

2. A man bought 650 pastries for a party.
   There were 39 pastries left after the party.
   How many pastries were eaten during the party?

3. The difference between two numbers is 48.
   If the greater number is 126, what is the smaller number?

4. Mr. Ray paid $450 for a television set.
   He still had $450 left.
   How much money did he have at first?

5. 429 concert tickets were sold on Sunday.
   64 more concert tickets were sold on Sunday than
   on Saturday.
   How many tickets were sold on Saturday?

6. Ryan had 35 tickets to sell.
   He sold 15 tickets yesterday and 9 tickets today.
   (a) How many tickets did he sell on the two days?
   (b) How many tickets were **not** sold?

7. David collected 830 stamps.
   Peter collected 177 fewer stamps than David.
   (a) How many stamps did Peter collect?
   (b) How many stamps did they collect altogether?

5 Adding Ones, Tens, Hundreds and Thousands

Find the sum of 2803 and 1443.

```
  2 8 0 3
+ 1 4 4 3
```

Estimate the answer by rounding to the nearest thousand.

```
2 8 0 3 ⟶    3 0 0 0
1 4 4 3 ⟶ +  1 0 0 0
             4 0 0 0
```

The answer should be about 4000.

As there are more than 10 hundreds, we change 10 hundreds for 1 thousand.

Add the ones.
```
  2 8 0 3
+ 1 4 4 3
        6
```

Add the tens.
```
  2 8 0 3
+ 1 4 4 3
      4 6
```

Add the hundreds.
```
   ¹
  2 8 0 3
+ 1 4 4 3
    2 4 6
```

Add the thousands.
```
   ¹
  2 8 0 3
+ 1 4 4 3
  4 2 4 6
```

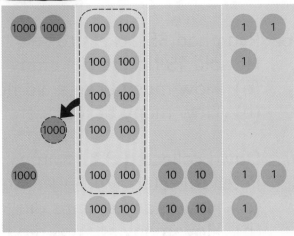

Is the answer reasonable?

1. Find the value of
   (a) 4263 + 5
   (b) 4263 + 20
   (c) 4263 + 400
   (d) 4263 + 3000
   (e) 4263 + 425
   (f) 4263 + 3425

2. 2048 + 2 =

```
    2 0 4 8
 +        2
 _____
```

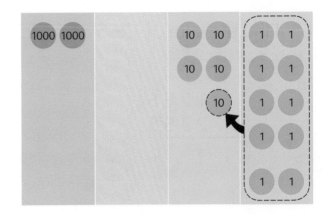

3. 5840 + 60 =

```
    5 8 4 0
 +      6 0
 _____
```

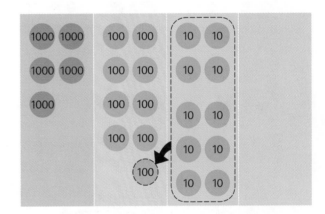

4. 3700 + 300 =

```
    3 7 0 0
 +    3 0 0
 _____
```

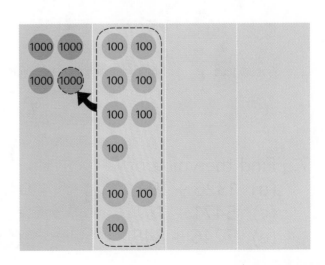

5. Find the value of
   (a) 1028 + 234   (b) 2409 + 1245
   (c) 4190 + 649   (d) 3260 + 4282
   (e) 6204 + 993   (f) 5402 + 2960

Exercise 11, pages 48-50

6. Find the sum of 1266 and 2355.

```
  1 2 6 6
+ 2 3 5 5
```

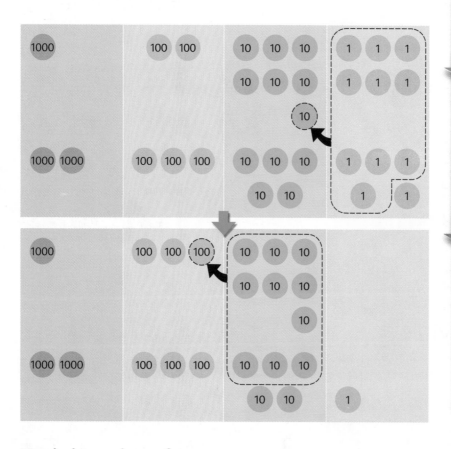

Add the ones.
```
    ¹
  1 2 6 6
+ 2 3 5 5
        1
```

Add the tens.
```
  ¹ ¹
  1 2 6 6
+ 2 3 5 5
      2 1
```

Add the hundreds.
```
  ¹ ¹
  1 2 6 6
+ 2 3 5 5
    6 2 1
```

Add the thousands.
```
  ¹ ¹
  1 2 6 6
+ 2 3 5 5
  3 6 2 1
```

7. Find the value of
   (a) 1326 + 194   (b) 3762 + 5158
   (c) 5471 + 787   (d) 6942 + 1095
   (e) 7246 + 845   (f) 4653 + 2729

8. Find the sum of 3589 and 2443.

$$3589 + 2443 = $$

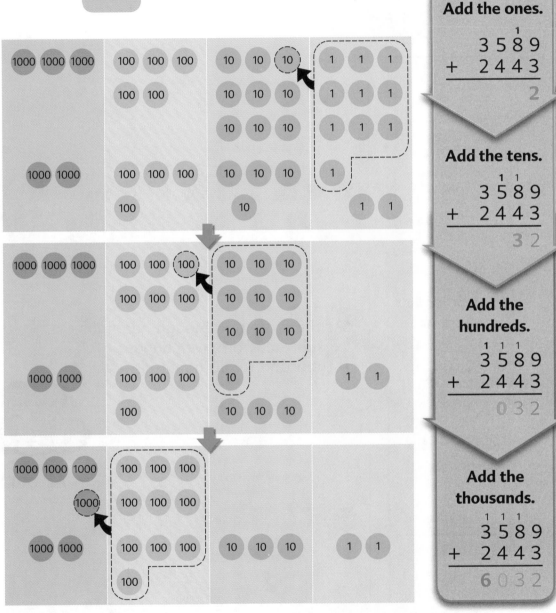

Add the ones.

$$
\begin{array}{r}
\overset{1}{3}589 \\
+\ 2443 \\
\hline
2
\end{array}
$$

Add the tens.

$$
\begin{array}{r}
\overset{1}{3}\overset{1}{5}89 \\
+\ 2443 \\
\hline
32
\end{array}
$$

Add the hundreds.

$$
\begin{array}{r}
\overset{1}{3}\overset{1}{5}\overset{1}{8}9 \\
+\ 2443 \\
\hline
032
\end{array}
$$

Add the thousands.

$$
\begin{array}{r}
\overset{1}{3}\overset{1}{5}\overset{1}{8}9 \\
+\ 2443 \\
\hline
6032
\end{array}
$$

9. Find the value of each of the following.
   Use estimation to see if your answers are reasonable.

   (a) 4697 + 1316   (b) 3587 + 3813
   (c) 2908 + 5892   (d) 2824 + 2576

Exercise 12, pages 51–52

6 Subtracting Ones, Tens, Hundreds and Thousands

Find the difference between 3246 and 1634.

$$
\begin{array}{r}
3\,2\,4\,6 \\
-\ 1\,6\,3\,4 \\
\hline
\end{array}
$$

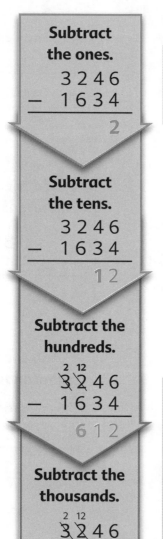

Subtract the ones.

$$
\begin{array}{r}
3\,2\,4\,6 \\
-\ 1\,6\,3\,4 \\
\hline
2
\end{array}
$$

Subtract the tens.

$$
\begin{array}{r}
3\,2\,4\,6 \\
-\ 1\,6\,3\,4 \\
\hline
1\,2
\end{array}
$$

As there are not enough hundreds to subtract from, we change 1 thousand for 10 hundreds.

Subtract the hundreds.

$$
\begin{array}{r}
\overset{2}{\cancel{3}}\,\overset{12}{2}\,4\,6 \\
-\ 1\,6\,3\,4 \\
\hline
6\,1\,2
\end{array}
$$

Subtract the thousands.

$$
\begin{array}{r}
\overset{2}{\cancel{3}}\,\overset{12}{2}\,4\,6 \\
-\ 1\,6\,3\,4 \\
\hline
1\,6\,1\,2
\end{array}
$$

1. Find the value of
   (a) 6847 − 3
   (b) 6847 − 20
   (c) 6847 − 500
   (d) 6847 − 4000
   (e) 6847 − 523
   (f) 6847 − 4523

2. 5340 − 6 =

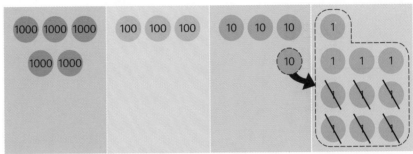

3. 4500 − 80 =

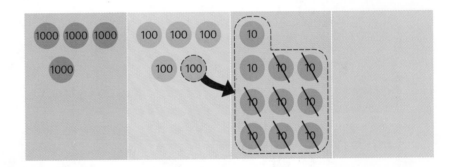

4. 7000 − 300 =

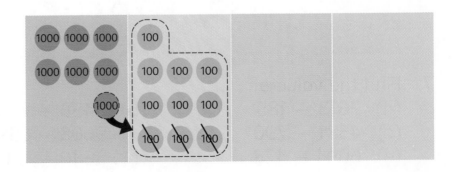

55

5. Find the value of
    (a) 4821 − 514
    (b) 5645 − 1317
    (c) 6743 − 461
    (d) 8769 − 3292
    (e) 9674 − 853
    (f) 7356 − 4731

Exercise 13, pages 53-54

6. Find the difference between 2435 and 1268.

```
    2 4 3 5
  − 1 2 6 8
```

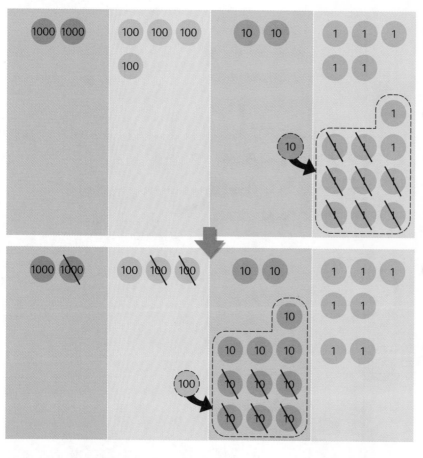

Subtract
the ones.

```
        2 15
    2 4 ̶3 ̶5
  − 1 2 6 8
          7
```

Subtract
the tens.

```
      3 12 15
    2 ̶4 ̶3 ̶5
  − 1 2 6 8
        6 7
```

Subtract the
hundreds.

```
      3 12 15
    2 ̶4 ̶3 ̶5
  − 1 2 6 8
      1 6 7
```

Subtract the
thousands.

```
      3 12 15
    2 ̶4 ̶3 ̶5
  − 1 2 6 8
    1 1 6 7
```

7. Find the value of
    (a) 7613 − 185
    (b) 8450 − 4262
    (c) 4581 − 790
    (d) 9608 − 6894
    (e) 6094 − 428
    (f) 3640 − 1807

8. Find the difference between 5243 and 2787.

$$\begin{array}{r} 5\,2\,4\,3 \\ -\ 2\,7\,8\,7 \\ \hline \end{array}$$

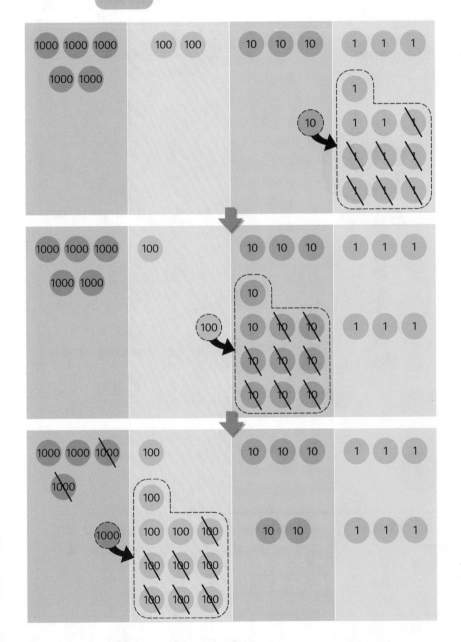

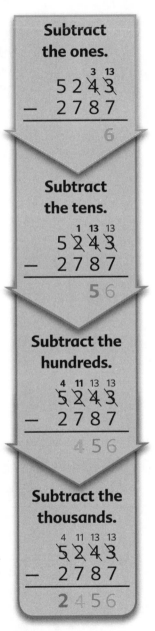

Subtract the ones.

$$\begin{array}{r} 5\,2\,4\,\overset{3\ \ 13}{\cancel{3}} \\ -\ 2\,7\,8\,7 \\ \hline 6 \end{array}$$

Subtract the tens.

$$\begin{array}{r} 5\,\overset{1}{\cancel{2}}\,\overset{13}{\cancel{4}}\,\overset{13}{\cancel{3}} \\ -\ 2\,7\,8\,7 \\ \hline 5\,6 \end{array}$$

Subtract the hundreds.

$$\begin{array}{r} \overset{4}{\cancel{5}}\,\overset{11}{\cancel{2}}\,\overset{13}{\cancel{4}}\,\overset{13}{\cancel{3}} \\ -\ 2\,7\,8\,7 \\ \hline 4\,5\,6 \end{array}$$

Subtract the thousands.

$$\begin{array}{r} \overset{4}{\cancel{5}}\,\overset{11}{\cancel{2}}\,\overset{13}{\cancel{4}}\,\overset{13}{\cancel{3}} \\ -\ 2\,7\,8\,7 \\ \hline 2\,4\,5\,6 \end{array}$$

9. Find the value of each of the following.
   Use estimation to see if your answers are reasonable.
   (a) 9564 − 8467   (b) 6875 − 3996
   (c) 8353 − 3572   (d) 7165 − 5268

Exercise 14, pages 55-56

10. Find the difference between 6000 and 257.

$$
\begin{array}{r}
6\,0\,0\,0 \\
-\quad 2\,5\,7 \\
\hline
\end{array}
$$

Change 1 thousand for 9 hundreds, 9 tens and 10 ones.

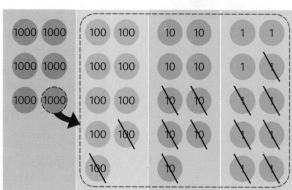

Subtract the ones.

$$
\begin{array}{r}
{\scriptstyle 5\;9\;9\;10} \\
\not6\,\not0\,\not0\,\not0 \\
-\quad 2\,5\,7 \\
\hline
3
\end{array}
$$

Subtract the tens.

$$
\begin{array}{r}
{\scriptstyle 5\;9\;9\;10} \\
\not6\,\not0\,\not0\,\not0 \\
-\quad 2\,5\,7 \\
\hline
4\,3
\end{array}
$$

Subtract the hundreds.

$$
\begin{array}{r}
{\scriptstyle 5\;9\;9\;10} \\
\not6\,\not0\,\not0\,\not0 \\
-\quad 2\,5\,7 \\
\hline
7\,4\,3
\end{array}
$$

Subtract the thousands.

$$
\begin{array}{r}
{\scriptstyle 5\;9\;9\;10} \\
\not6\,\not0\,\not0\,\not0 \\
-\quad 2\,5\,7 \\
\hline
5\,7\,4\,3
\end{array}
$$

11. $6004 - 2678 = $

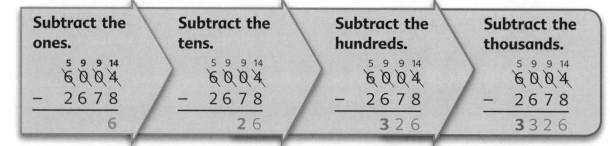

Subtract the ones.	**Subtract the tens.**	**Subtract the hundreds.**	**Subtract the thousands.**
$\begin{array}{r} {\scriptstyle 5\;9\;9\;14} \\ \not6\,\not0\,\not0\,\not4 \\ -\ 2\,6\,7\,8 \\ \hline 6 \end{array}$	$\begin{array}{r} {\scriptstyle 5\;9\;9\;14} \\ \not6\,\not0\,\not0\,\not4 \\ -\ 2\,6\,7\,8 \\ \hline 2\,6 \end{array}$	$\begin{array}{r} {\scriptstyle 5\;9\;9\;14} \\ \not6\,\not0\,\not0\,\not4 \\ -\ 2\,6\,7\,8 \\ \hline 3\,2\,6 \end{array}$	$\begin{array}{r} {\scriptstyle 5\;9\;9\;14} \\ \not6\,\not0\,\not0\,\not4 \\ -\ 2\,6\,7\,8 \\ \hline 3\,3\,2\,6 \end{array}$

12. Find the value of
    (a) $4000 - 392$ (b) $7002 - 4847$
    (c) $3020 - 2430$ (d) $5000 - 2074$

13. 5200 − 948 = ☐

$$
\begin{array}{r}
5\,2\,0\,0 \\
-\quad 9\,4\,8 \\
\hline
\end{array}
$$

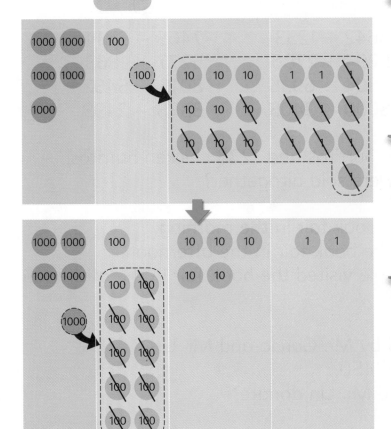

Subtract the ones.

$$
\begin{array}{r}
5\,\overset{1}{\cancel{2}}\,\overset{9}{\cancel{0}}\,\overset{10}{\cancel{0}} \\
-\quad 9\,4\,8 \\
\hline
2
\end{array}
$$

Subtract the tens.

$$
\begin{array}{r}
5\,\overset{1}{\cancel{2}}\,\overset{9}{\cancel{0}}\,\overset{10}{\cancel{0}} \\
-\quad 9\,4\,8 \\
\hline
5\,2
\end{array}
$$

Subtract the hundreds.

$$
\begin{array}{r}
\overset{4}{\cancel{5}}\,\overset{11}{\cancel{2}}\,\overset{9}{\cancel{0}}\,\overset{10}{\cancel{0}} \\
-\quad 9\,4\,8 \\
\hline
2\,5\,2
\end{array}
$$

Subtract the thousands.

$$
\begin{array}{r}
\overset{4}{\cancel{5}}\,\overset{11}{\cancel{2}}\,\overset{9}{\cancel{0}}\,\overset{10}{\cancel{0}} \\
-\quad 9\,4\,8 \\
\hline
4\,2\,5\,2
\end{array}
$$

14. Find the value of each of the following.
    Use estimation to see if your answers are reasonable.
    (a) 8007 − 3429   (b) 6900 − 745
    (c) 9403 − 4275   (d) 5302 − 4618

15. Find the value of each of the following.
    Check your answers with addition.
    (a) 7063 − 5476
    (b) 10,000 − 5721

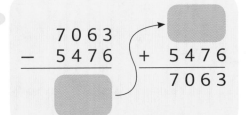

$$
\begin{array}{r}
7\,0\,6\,3 \\
-\quad 5\,4\,7\,6 \\
\hline
\end{array}
\qquad
\begin{array}{r}
\\
+\quad 5\,4\,7\,6 \\
\hline
7\,0\,6\,3
\end{array}
$$

59

Exercise 15, pages 57-58

Find the value of each of the following. Use estimation to see if your answers are reasonable.

	(a)	(b)	(c)
1.	4329 + 5450	3642 + 1253	7465 − 3214
2.	6347 + 2613	5294 + 2706	5277 − 1863
3.	4389 + 3175	7804 − 6935	8016 − 5452
4.	3490 + 1844	8000 − 3405	3378 − 2499

5. A shop sold 957 beef burritos and 1238 chicken burritos. How many burritos were sold altogether?

6. 1730 people visited a book fair in the morning.
   2545 people visited the book fair in the afternoon.
   How many more people visited the book fair in the afternoon than in the morning?

7. $2937 were donated by Mr. Garcia and Mr. Lin.
   Mr. Garcia donated $1450.
   How much money did Mr. Lin donate?

8. Alice saved $2900.
   She saved $1567 less than her brother.
   How much did her brother save?

Find the value of each of the following. Use estimation to see if your answers are reasonable.

	(a)	(b)	(c)
1.	6203 + 977	2645 + 3875	8300 − 4251
2.	5472 + 4415	4975 + 1928	9613 − 5357
3.	2446 + 6596	7042 − 5170	3142 − 1455
4.	3421 + 4282	9000 − 6571	7173 − 3654

5. There were 2055 men and 1637 women at a concert. How many people were there altogether?

6. There are 1206 students in a school. 47 of them were absent yesterday. How many students were present?

7. Out of 2316 tickets sold, 1548 tickets were for a football game. The rest were for a basketball game. How many tickets for the basketball game were sold?

8. The table shows the prices of two pianos. How much cheaper is Piano B than Piano A?

Piano A	$2005
Piano B	$1542

9. In a school, there are 1225 girls and 904 boys.
   (a) How many fewer boys are there than girls?
   (b) How many students are there altogether?

7 Two-step Word Problems

Jamie picked 17 flowers and Lindsey picked 12.
They gave away 20 of the flowers.
How many flowers were left?

> Find the total number of flowers they picked altogether first.

$$17 + 12 = 29$$

They picked 29 flowers altogether.

$$29 - 20 = \boxed{}$$

$\boxed{}$ flowers were left.

1. 125 children took part in a mathematics competition.
    54 of them were girls.
    How many more boys than girls were there?

Find the total number of boys first.

$$125 - 54 = 71$$

There were 71 boys.

$$71 - 54 = \boxed{}$$

There were $\boxed{}$ more boys than girls.

2. Ali collected 137 stamps.
    He collected 27 fewer stamps than his sister.
    How many stamps did they collect altogether?

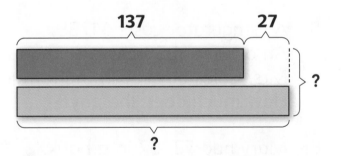

$$137 + 27 = 164$$

Ali's sister collected 164 stamps.

$$137 + 164 = \boxed{}$$

They collected $\boxed{}$ stamps altogether.

Exercise 16, pages 59-61

1. A farmer collected 1930 chicken eggs.
   He collected 859 fewer duck eggs than chicken eggs.
   How many eggs did he collect altogether?

2. 4100 children took part in an art competition.
   2680 of them were boys.
   How many more boys than girls were there?

3. Ali made 1050 sticks of chicken satay and
   950 sticks of beef satay.
   After he sold all his sticks of satay, he made
   765 more sticks.
   How many sticks of satay did he make altogether?

4. Mark earned $3915.
   He spent $1268 on food and $1380 on rent and transport.
   How much did he have left?

5. A refrigerator costs $1739.
   An oven is $850 cheaper than the refrigerator.
   Mrs. Coles buys both the refrigerator and the oven.
   How much does she pay?

6. Mary had $2467 in a bank.
   She deposited another $133.
   How much more money must she deposit if she wants to
   have $3000 in the bank?

REVIEW 2

1. Write the numbers in standard form.
   (a) one thousand, three hundred seventy-six
   (b) four thousand, five

2. Write 5900 in words.

3. Write 4091 in thousands, hundreds, tens and ones.

4. Find the missing numbers.
   (a) $1000 + 700 + 30 + 6 = \boxed{}$

   (b) $7000 + 500 + 4 = \boxed{}$

   (c) $3000 + \boxed{} = 3090$

   (d) $6000 + \boxed{} + 2 = 6802$

   (e) $4243 = 4000 + 200 + 40 + \boxed{}$

   (f) $4907 - \boxed{} = 4007$

5. Write > or < in place of each ◯.
   (a) 3590 ◯ 3509

   (b) 9989 ◯ 9998

   (c) 7080 ◯ 7100

   (d) 2000 ◯ 10,000

6. Which is the smallest number in each of the following?
   (a) 9909,   9099,   9990
   (b) 8544,   8454,   8445

7. Arrange these numbers in order, beginning with the greatest.

208   989   1260   1098

8. (a) In 6243, the digit ⬜ is in the **tens place**.

Its value is ⬜ .

(b) In 5029, the digit ⬜ is in the **hundreds place**.

Its value is ⬜ .

9. Write the next three numbers for each of the following number patterns.

(a) 5612,   5622,   5632,   ⬜ ,   ⬜ ,   ⬜

(b) 1800,   1900,   2000,   ⬜ ,   ⬜ ,   ⬜

(c) 4056,   5056,   6056,   ⬜ ,   ⬜ ,   ⬜

10. (a) Estimate the value of 469 + 37 by rounding to the nearest ten.
    (b) Estimate the value of 4598 − 432 by rounding to the nearest hundred.
    (c) Estimate the value of 7087 − 2592 by rounding to the nearest thousand.

11. Find the value of 17 + 48 + 22 + 61.

Find the value of each of the following:

	(a)	(b)	(c)
12.	730 + 313	305 + 179	265 + 161
13.	724 + 184	310 + 184	668 + 475
14.	746 − 316	310 − 187	600 − 382
15.	470 − 371	627 − 298	374 − 361

16. Find the missing numbers.

    (a) 3984 + 2653 = ▢

    (b) 7045 − 999 = ▢

    (c) 5684 + ▢ = 7002

    (d) 6032 − ▢ = 1532

17. Mr. Wallace earned $3265.
    His wife earned $2955.
    How much more money did he earn than his wife?

18. 1147 people went to Sentosa by cable car.
    3996 more people went to Sentosa by ferry than by cable car.
    How many people went to Sentosa by ferry?

19. Mr. Johnson had $5000.
    He spent $2572 on a computer and $955 on a television set.
    (a) How much money did he spend?
    (b) How much money did he have left?

20. There are 4608 members in a club.
    2745 of them are men.
    855 are women.
    The rest are children.
    How many children are there?

21. Miss Li saved $1035.
    Miss Wang saved $278 more than Miss Li.
    Miss Wu saved $105 less than Miss Wang.
    How much did Miss Wu save?

Review 2, pages 62-65

3 MULTIPLICATION AND DIVISION

1 Looking Back

1	2	3	4	5	6	7	8	9	10

2	4	6	8			14	16		20

3	6	9			18	21		27	30

4	8	12	16			28		36	

5	10	15		25	30			45	50

10	20			50	60	70	80		100

2 multiplied by 4 is 8.
What is 2 multiplied by 5?

68

1. A dog has four legs.
   How many legs do 7 dogs have?

Number of dogs	1	2	3	4	5	6	7
Number of legs	4	8	12	16	20	24	

$4 + 4 + 4 + 4 + 4 + 4 + 4 =$ ▢

$7 \times 4 =$ ▢

7 dogs have ▢ legs.

I can multiply the number of dogs by 4.

2. A toy car costs $5.
   How much do 8 toy cars cost?

Number of cars	1	2	3	4	5	6	7	8
Cost	$5	$10	$15	$20	$25	$30	$	$

The cost equals the number of cars multiplied by 5.

$8 \times 5 =$ ▢

8 toy cars cost $▢.

3. How many dimes can you trade for 9 dollars?

Dollars	1	2	3	4	5	6	7	8	9
Dimes	10	20	30	40	50	60			

The number of dimes equals the number of dollars

multiplied by [ ].

9 × 10 = [ ]

I can trade [ ] dimes for 9 dollars.

Exercise 1, pages 66-68

4. Complete the number sentences.

4 × 3 = [ ]   3 × 4 = [ ]

4 + 4 + 4 = [ ]   3 + 3 + 3 + 3 = [ ]

5. How many stars are there on each pair of cards?

(a)

$3 \times 2 = $

(b)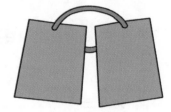

$2 \times 2 = $

(c)

$1 \times 2 = $

(d)

$0 \times 2 = $

6. A player threw 3 rings over the post.
For each ring that was thrown in, the player scored 2 points.
How many points were scored in each of the following?

(a)

$2 \times 3 = $

(b)

$2 \times 2 = $

(c)

$2 \times 1 = $

(d)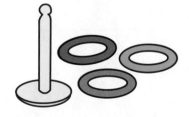

$2 \times 0 = $

7. $1 \times 0 = 0$ $3 \times 0 = 0$ $5 \times 0 = 0$

   $2 \times 0 =$ 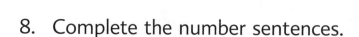 $10 \times 0 =$ $100 \times 0 =$

   Any number multiplied by 0 equals .

8. Complete the number sentences.

   (a) $1 \times 1 =$ (b) $2 \times 1 =$ (c) $3 \times 1 =$

   (d) $1 \times 4 =$ (e) $5 \times 1 =$ (f) $1 \times 10 =$

9. (a) $914 \times 1 =$ (b) $914 \times 0 =$

1 multiplied by any number equals that number.

0 multiplied by any number equals 0.

Exercise 2, pages 69-71

10.

   $5 \times 4 =$ $\boxed{} \div 4 = 5$

   $4 \times 5 =$ $\boxed{} \div 5 = 4$

11. What are the missing numbers?

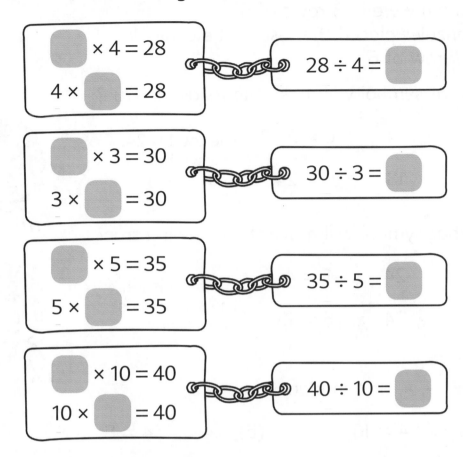

□ × 4 = 28
4 × □ = 28
28 ÷ 4 = □

□ × 3 = 30
3 × □ = 30
30 ÷ 3 = □

□ × 5 = 35
5 × □ = 35
35 ÷ 5 = □

□ × 10 = 40
10 × □ = 40
40 ÷ 10 = □

12. Find the missing numbers.

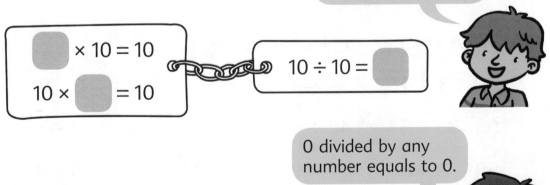

A number divided by itself is always 1.

□ × 10 = 10
10 × □ = 10
10 ÷ 10 = □

0 divided by any number equals to 0.

□ × 2 = 0
2 × □ = 0
0 ÷ 2 = □

Exercise 3, pages 72-75

13. There were 24 chairs.
    18 of them were in 3 rows of 6.
    Mr. Gonzales placed the rest of the chairs in
    another row of 6.

    (a) What symbol will make the following true?

    4 ⬤ 6 = 24

    18 ⬤ 6 = 24

    The total is 24.
    The symbol has
    to be + or ×.

    (b) What symbol will make the following true?

    24 ⬤ 6 = 4

    24 ⬤ 6 = 18

    The total is 24.
    The symbol has
    to be − or ÷.

14. Write **+**, **−**, **×**, or **÷** in place of each ⬤.

    (a) 4 ⬤ 4 = 16   (b) 4 ⬤ 4 = 8

    (c) 12 ⬤ 4 = 8   (d) 12 ⬤ 3 = 4

    (e) 13 ⬤ 7 = 2 × 3   (f) 6 × 4 = 8 ⬤ 3

15. Write **>**, **<**, or **=** in place of each ⬤.

    (a) 3 × 4 ⬤ 4 × 3   (b) 2 × 6 ⬤ 6 × 3

    (c) 35 ÷ 5 ⬤ 40 ÷ 4   (d) 5 × 8 ⬤ 35 + 5

    (e) 3 × 6 ⬤ 2 × 9   (f) 24 ÷ 3 ⬤ 3 × 4

74

Exercise 4, pages 76-78

16. There are 8 buttons on each card.
    How many buttons are there on 5 cards?

Multiply 8 by 5.

$8 \times 5 = $

There are ⬜ buttons altogether.

17. Nicole bought 3 packets of strawberries.
    There were 8 strawberries in each packet.
    How many strawberries did she buy altogether?

$3 \times 8 = $ ⬜

Nicole bought ⬜ strawberries altogether.

18. A tailor used 21 m of cloth to make dresses.
    She used 3 m of cloth for each dress.
    How many dresses did she make?

    $21 \div 3 = \boxed{}$

    She made $\boxed{}$ dresses.

    $3 \times \boxed{} = 21$

    $21 \div 3 = \boxed{}$

19. Sean arranged 24 toy soldiers in 4 rows.
    There were an equal number of toy soldiers in each row.
    How many toy soldiers were there in each row?

    $24 \div 4 = \boxed{}$

    There were $\boxed{}$ toy soldiers in each row.

20. For each word problem, state whether you multiply or divide.
    Then, solve the problem.

    (a) Denise saved $5 a week for 8 weeks.
        How much did she save altogether?

    (b) Ashley paid $18 for 3 kg of cherries.
        What was the cost of 1 kg of cherries?

    (c) Wendy baked 6 cakes.
        She put 10 cherries on each cake.
        How many cherries did she use altogether?

    (d) David bought 4 pineapples at $3 each.
        How much did he pay altogether?

    (e) There were 27 desks to clean.
        3 boys shared the work equally.
        How many desks did each boy clean?

    (f) 3 children made 24 birthday cards altogether.
        Each child made the same number of cards.
        How many cards did each child make?

76

Exercise 5, pages 79-80

2 More Word Problems

There are 9 blue flowers.
There are 3 times as many red flowers as blue flowers.
How many red flowers are there?

There are more red flowers than blue flowers.

Multiply 9 by 3.

9 × 3 = 27

There are ___ red flowers.

1. Melanie has $16.
   She has twice as much money as Sally.
   How much money does Sally have?

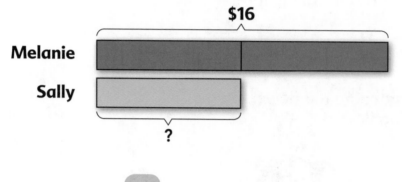

$16

Melanie

Sally

?

Divide 16 by 2.

$16 \div 2 = $

Sally has $.

2. 4 children bought a present for $28.
   They shared the cost equally.
   How much did each child pay?

$28

?

$28 \div 4 = $

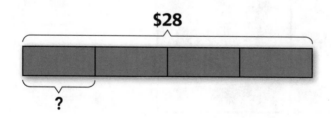

4 units = $28
1 unit = $28 ÷ 4

Each child paid $.

3. 5 children shared the cost of a book equally.
Each of them paid $6.
What was the cost of the book?

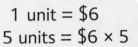

1 unit = $6
5 units = $6 × 5

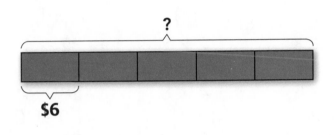

?

$6

$6 × 5 =$ ▢

The cost of the book was $ ▢.

Exercise 6, pages 81-83

4. A farmer has 7 ducks.
He has 5 times as many chickens as ducks.
How many more chickens than ducks does he have?

Find the number
of chickens first.

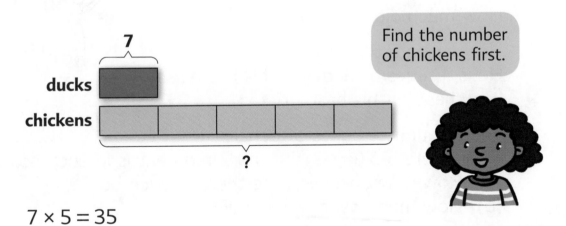

7

ducks

chickens

?

$7 × 5 = 35$

He has 35 chickens.

$35 - 7 =$ ▢

He has ▢ more chickens than ducks.

79

Exercise 7, pages 84-85

Find the value of each of the following:

	(a)	(b)	(c)	(d)
1.	6 × 2	24 ÷ 3	2 × 7	32 ÷ 4
2.	7 × 3	14 ÷ 2	5 × 6	20 ÷ 5
3.	3 × 4	25 ÷ 5	4 × 8	28 ÷ 4
4.	7 × 5	16 ÷ 4	10 × 2	60 ÷ 10
5.	9 × 10	70 ÷ 10	3 × 9	36 ÷ 4

6. There are 30 chairs in the classroom.
   They are arranged in 6 equal rows.
   How many chairs are there in each row?

7. A toy car costs $6.
   A train set costs 5 times as much as the toy car.
   What is the cost of the train set?

8. Mrs. Lee bought 10 towels.
   Each towel cost $8.
   How much did she pay?

9. Harry weighs 36 kg.
   He is 4 times as heavy as his brother.
   How heavy is his brother?

10. Emily bought 4 boxes of pencils.
    There were 5 blue pencils and 3 red pencils in each box.
    (a) How many pencils were there in each box?
    (b) How many pencils did Emily buy?

11. Miss Levinsky graded 5 sets of 8 journals in the morning.
    She graded 30 journals in the afternoon.
    (a) How many journals did she grade in the morning?
    (b) How many journals did she grade altogether?

12. There are 9 red balloons.
    There are 3 times as many blue balloons as red balloons.
    How many balloons are there altogether?

PRACTICE B

Find the value of each of the following:

	(a)	(b)	(c)	(d)
1.	1 × 5	16 ÷ 2	6 × 3	24 ÷ 4
2.	9 × 2	12 ÷ 4	5 × 7	8 ÷ 8
3.	3 × 3	0 ÷ 5	3 × 8	15 ÷ 3
4.	8 × 4	90 ÷ 10	2 × 0	50 ÷ 10
5.	0 × 4	21 ÷ 3	4 × 6	0 ÷ 2

6. Andy earned $10 a day.
    He worked for 7 days.
    How much did he earn altogether?

7. Miss Meyer bought 15 kg of rice.
    She bought 3 times as much rice as sugar.
    How many kilograms of sugar did she buy?

8. Devi practised on the piano for 2 hours each day.
    How many hours did she practice in 7 days?

9. Lynn poured 16 qt of syrup equally into 4 bottles.
    How many quarts of syrup were there in each bottle?

10. Melissa has 6 postcards.
    Sally has 3 times as many postcards as Melissa.
    How many more postcards does Sally have than Melissa?

11. Brian has 6 goldfish.
    He has 5 times as many guppies as goldfish.
    If he puts his guppies equally into 3 tanks,
    how many guppies are there in each tank?

12. Ryan bought 18 pencils.
    He bought twice as many pencils as pens.
    How much did he pay for the pens if each pen cost $3?

③ Multiplying Ones, Tens, Hundreds and Thousands

1 1 1 1
1 1 1 1
1 1 1 1

$4 \times 3 = 12$

Multiply 4 ones by 3:
4 ones × 3 = 12 ones

10 10 10 10
10 10 10 10
10 10 10 10

$40 \times 3 = $ ☐

Multiply 4 tens by 3:
4 tens × 3 = 12 tens

100 100 100 100
100 100 100 100
100 100 100 100

$400 \times 3 = $ ☐

Multiply 4 hundreds by 3:
4 hundreds × 3 = 12 hundreds

$4 \times 3 = 12$

$$
\begin{array}{r}
4 \\
\times \quad 3 \\
\hline
12
\end{array}
$$

12 ones

When we multiply 4 by 3, the **product** is 12.

$40 \times 3 = 120$

$$
\begin{array}{r}
4\mathbf{0} \\
\times \quad 3 \\
\hline
12\mathbf{0}
\end{array}
$$

12 tens

120 is the **product of 40 and 3**.

$400 \times 3 = 1200$

$$
\begin{array}{r}
4\mathbf{00} \\
\times \quad 3 \\
\hline
12\mathbf{00}
\end{array}
$$

12 hundreds

1. Find the value of

(a)	9×5	(b)	90×5	(c)	900×5
(d)	5×9	(e)	50×9	(f)	500×9
(g)	6×5	(h)	60×5	(i)	600×5
(j)	20×3	(k)	200×3	(l)	2000×3

2. A bookseller sold 30 books on the first day.
   On the second day, he sold 8 times as many books as
   on the first day.
   How many books did he sell on the second day?

3 tens × 8 = [   ] tens

30 × 8 = [   ]

He sold [   ] books on the second day.

3. Find the product.
   (a) 20 × 9   (b) 3 × 80   (c) 4 × 500   (d) 200 × 5
   (e) 40 × 6   (f) 5 × 10   (g) 5 × 800   (h) 400 × 4
   (i) 50 × 2   (j) 4 × 30   (k) 8 × 100   (l) 300 × 5

Exercise 8, pages 86-87

4. Multiply 12 by 4.

$$\begin{array}{r} 1\,2 \\ \times\ \ \ 4 \\ \hline \end{array}$$

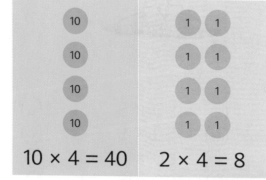

10 × 4 = 40   2 × 4 = 8

12 × 4 = 40 + 8

Multiply the
ones by 4.

$$\begin{array}{r} 1\,2 \\ \times\ \ \ 4 \\ \hline 8 \end{array}$$

Multiply the
tens by 4.

$$\begin{array}{r} 1\,2 \\ \times\ \ \ 4 \\ \hline 4\,8 \end{array}$$

84

5. Multiply 42 by 3.

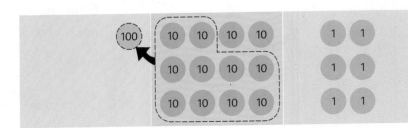

Multiply the ones by 3.

```
   4 2
 ×   3
─────────
       6
```

Multiply the tens by 3.

```
   4 2
 ×   3
─────────
   1 2 6
```

Exercise 9, pages 88-90

6. Multiply 24 by 3.

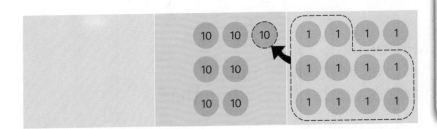

Multiply the ones by 3.

```
     1
   2 4
 ×   3
─────────
       2
```

Multiply the tens by 3.

```
     1
   2 4
 ×   3
─────────
     7 2
```

7. Multiply 34 by 3.

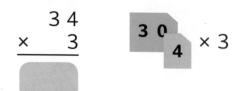

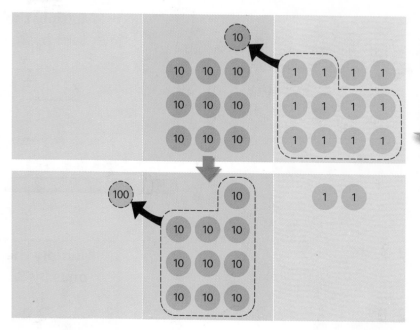

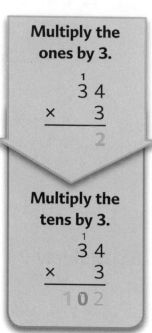

Multiply the
ones by 3.

$$
\begin{array}{r}
\overset{1}{3}\,4 \\
\times \quad 3 \\
\hline
2
\end{array}
$$

Multiply the
tens by 3.

$$
\begin{array}{r}
\overset{1}{3}\,4 \\
\times \quad 3 \\
\hline
1\,0\,2
\end{array}
$$

8. Find the product.
   (a) 81 × 2   (b) 16 × 3   (c) 3 × 37
   (d) 52 × 4   (e) 23 × 4   (f) 5 × 45
   (g) 63 × 3   (h) 24 × 5   (i) 4 × 38

9. Ming had 4 rolls of film.
   He took 24 pictures with each roll.
   How many pictures did he take altogether?

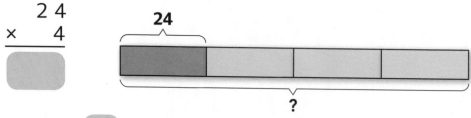

He took ☐ pictures altogether.

10. There are 5 rows of tiles.
There are 56 tiles in each row.
How many tiles are there altogether?

$$\begin{array}{r} 5\,6 \\ \times\quad\ 5 \\ \hline \end{array}$$

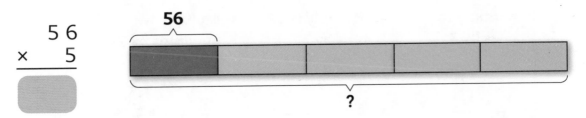

There are ⬚ tiles altogether.

Exercise 10, pages 91-93

11. $3 \times 342 =$ ⬚

$$\begin{array}{r} 3\,4\,2 \\ \times\quad\ \ 3 \\ \hline \end{array}$$

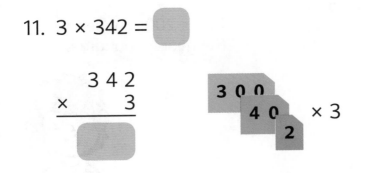

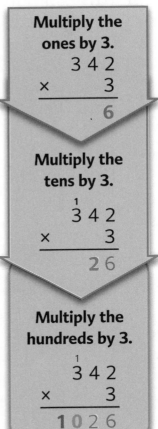

Multiply the
ones by 3.

$$\begin{array}{r} 3\,4\,2 \\ \times\quad\ \ 3 \\ \hline 6 \end{array}$$

Multiply the
tens by 3.

$$\begin{array}{r} {}^{1}3\,4\,2 \\ \times\quad\ \ 3 \\ \hline 2\,6 \end{array}$$

Multiply the
hundreds by 3.

$$\begin{array}{r} {}^{1}3\,4\,2 \\ \times\quad\ \ 3 \\ \hline 1\,0\,2\,6 \end{array}$$

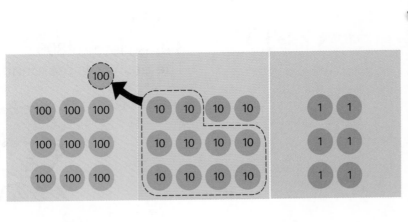

12. Find the product of 245 and 3.

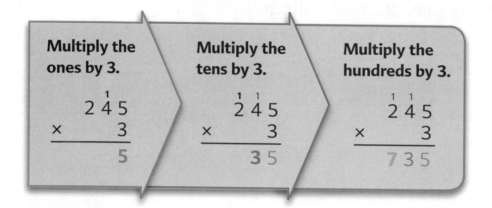

Multiply the ones by 3.

$$\begin{array}{r} 2\overset{1}{4}5 \\ \times3 \\ \hline 5 \end{array}$$

Multiply the tens by 3.

$$\begin{array}{r} \overset{1}{2}\overset{1}{4}5 \\ \times3 \\ \hline 35 \end{array}$$

Multiply the hundreds by 3.

$$\begin{array}{r} \overset{1}{2}\overset{1}{4}5 \\ \times3 \\ \hline 735 \end{array}$$

13. (a) Estimate the value of 212 × 4.

212 is 200 rounded to the nearest hundred.

$200 \times 4 =$

The value of 212 × 4 is about .

(b) Find the value of 212 × 4.

$212 \times 4 =$

The value of 212 × 4 is .

$$\begin{array}{r} 2\,1\,2 \\ \times4 \\ \hline 8\,4\,8 \end{array}$$

848 is close to 800.
The answer is reasonable.

14. Find the product for each of the following.
    Use estimation to see if your answer is reasonable.

    (a) 214 × 2   (b) 323 × 3   (c) 4 × 231
    (d) 620 × 3   (e) 451 × 2   (f) 3 × 234
    (g) 289 × 3   (h) 704 × 5   (i) 5 × 436

Exercise 11, pages 94-95

15. 3 × 1612 =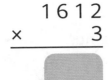

$$\begin{array}{r} 1\,6\,1\,2 \\ \times \qquad 3 \\ \hline \end{array}$$

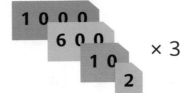

Multiply the ones by 3.

$$\begin{array}{r} 1\,6\,1\,2 \\ \times \qquad 3 \\ \hline 6 \end{array}$$

Multiply the tens by 3.

$$\begin{array}{r} 1\,6\,1\,2 \\ \times \qquad 3 \\ \hline 3\,6 \end{array}$$

Multiply the hundreds by 3.

$$\begin{array}{r} ^{1}\,\\ 1\,6\,1\,2 \\ \times \qquad 3 \\ \hline 8\,3\,6 \end{array}$$

Multiply the thousands by 3.

$$\begin{array}{r} ^{1}\,\\ 1\,6\,1\,2 \\ \times \qquad 3 \\ \hline 4\,8\,3\,6 \end{array}$$

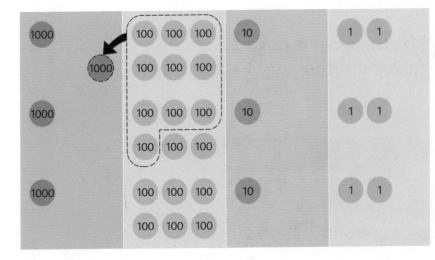

16. Find the product of 2987 and 3.

Multiply the ones by 3.	Multiply the tens by 3.	Multiply the hundreds by 3.	Multiply the thousands by 3.

² 2987
 ×   3
 ———
     1
	^{2 2} 2987
	 × 3
	 ———
	    61
		^{2 2 2} 2987
		 × 3
		 ———
		  961
			^{2 2 2} 2987
			 × 3
			 ———
			 8961

17. (a) Estimate the product of 3742 and 2.

$$4000 × 2 = \boxed{}$$

3742 is 4000 rounded to the nearest thousand.

The product of 3742 and 2 is about $\boxed{}$.

(b) Find the value of 3742 × 2.

Is the answer reasonable?

18. Find the product of each of the following. Use estimation to see if your answer is reasonable.

(a) 2701 × 3   (b) 1653 × 4   (c) 4289 × 2

19. There are 1250 staples in a box.
How many staples are there in 3 such boxes?

```
    1250
×      3
———————
  ▢
```

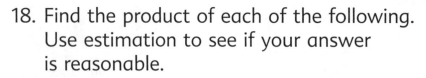

There are $\boxed{}$ staples in 3 boxes.

20. Drew has $598.
    Connie has 4 times as much money as Drew.
    (a) About how much money does Connie have?

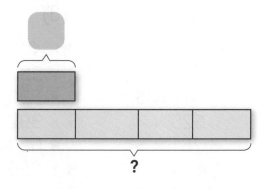

598 is 600
rounded to the
nearest hundred.

    Connie has about $ ____ .

(b) Exactly how much money does Connie have?

    Connie has exactly $ ____ .

Is the answer reasonable?

91

Exercise 12, pages 96-97

Find the value of each of the following:

	(a)	(b)	(c)	(d)
1.	60 × 4	6 × 50	200 × 6	7 × 400
2.	32 × 3	4 × 72	52 × 5	2 × 58
3.	300 × 4	3 × 312	419 × 5	4 × 550
4.	901 × 2	3 × 508	625 × 4	5 × 392
5.	614 × 5	4 × 432	781 × 5	3 × 623
6.	800 × 5	2 × 506	439 × 4	5 × 556
7.	2249 × 3	5 × 1361	1968 × 4	2 × 3704

8. Mel collected 76 stickers.
   Sue collected 3 times as many stickers as Mel.
   How many stickers did Sue collect?

9. A radio costs $262.
   A television set costs 4 times as much as the radio.
   (a) About how much does the television set cost?
   (b) Exactly how much does the television set cost?

10. Mrs. Owen bought 3 boxes of beads.
    There were 260 beads in each box.
    How many beads did she buy altogether?

11. One packet of raisins weighs 250 g.
    What is the total weight of 5 packets of raisins?

12. Cassey sold 680 eggs last week.
    She sold 4 times as many eggs this week as last week.
    How many eggs did she sell altogether?

13. The refrigerator costs 5 times as
    much as the toaster.
    What is the total cost of the refrigerator
    and the toaster?

$150

92

Find the value of each of the following:

	(a)	(b)	(c)	(d)
1.	30 × 8	9 × 20	400 × 7	4 × 500
2.	49 × 2	4 × 43	75 × 3	5 × 43
3.	12 × 2	3 × 14	16 × 5	4 × 18
4.	223 × 2	4 × 527	129 × 2	3 × 326
5.	252 × 3	4 × 763	372 × 5	3 × 284
6.	724 × 2	3 × 105	414 × 4	5 × 120
7.	3260 × 3	5 × 1415	1509 × 5	4 × 2309

8. Kate made 280 egg salad sandwiches for a party.
   She made 3 times as many chicken sandwiches as egg salad sandwiches.
   How many chicken sandwiches did she make?

9. There are 365 days in a year.
   How many days are there in 4 years?

10. A pilot flies 1050 hours in one month.
    (a) About how many hours will he fly in 5 months?
    (b) Exactly how many hours will he fly in 5 months?

11. One box of cornflakes weighs 350 g.
    Find the total weight of 2 boxes of cornflakes.

12. There were 30 cakes in one box.
    Wendy bought 4 such boxes of cakes.
    How much did she pay for the cakes if each cake cost $3?

13. There are 18 chairs in the first row.
    There are 25 chairs in each of the other 5 rows.
    How many chairs are there altogether?

4 Quotient and Remainder

Mandy has 14 toy soldiers.
She puts the toy soldiers equally into 4 tents.
How many soldiers are there in each tent?
How many soldiers are left over?

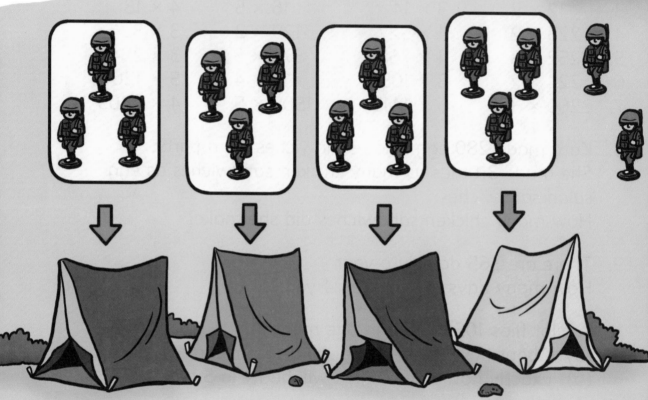

We write:
$14 \div 4 = 3 \, R \, 2$

$14 \div 4 = 3$ with remainder 2

There are ⬜ soldiers in each tent.

⬜ soldiers are left over.

$$\begin{array}{r} 3\,R\,2 \\ 4\overline{)14} \\ \underline{12} \\ 2 \end{array}$$

3×4

$14 - 12$

When 14 is divided by 4, the **quotient** is 3 and the **remainder** is 2.
We write the answer as 3 **R** 2.

Check your answer.

Quotient × 4 = 3 × 4 = 12
12 + remainder = 12 + 2 = **14**

Is 14 the number we divided?

1. Divide 9 by 2.

$$\begin{array}{r} 4\,R\,1 \\ 2\overline{)9} \\ \underline{8} \\ 1 \end{array}$$

$9 \div 2 = \boxed{}$

$4 \times 2 = 8$

$8 + 1 = \boxed{}$

2. Divide 12 by 2.

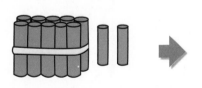

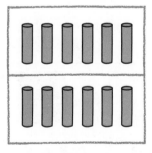

$$\begin{array}{r} 6 \\ 2\overline{)12} \\ \underline{12} \\ 0 \end{array}$$

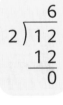

$12 \div 2 = \boxed{}$

$6 \times 2 = 12$

$12 + 0 = \boxed{}$

3. $28 \div 2 =$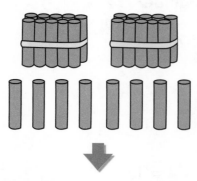

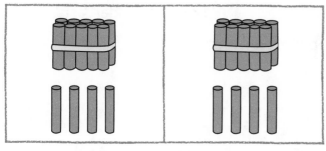

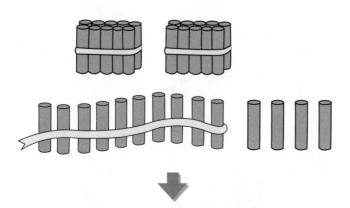

Divide the tens by 2.
2 tens ÷ 2 = 1 ten

$$2\overline{)28} \\ \underline{2}$$

with **1** above the 2.

Divide the ones by 2.
8 ones ÷ 2 = 4 ones

$$2\overline{)28} \\ \underline{2} \\ 8 \\ \underline{8} \\ 0$$

with **14** above.

4. $34 \div 2 =$

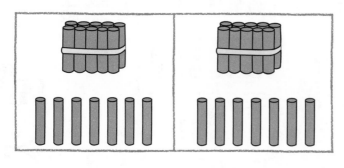

Divide the tens by 2.
3 tens ÷ 2 = 1 ten
with remainder 1 ten

$$2\overline{)34} \\ \underline{2} \\ 1$$

Divide the ones by 2.
14 ones ÷ 2 = 7 ones

$$2\overline{)34} \\ \underline{2} \\ 14 \\ \underline{14} \\ 0$$

5. $73 \div 2 = \boxed{}$

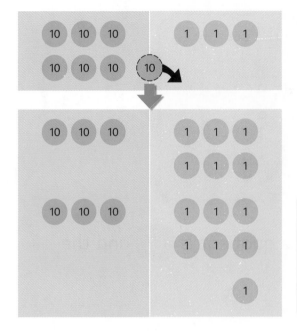

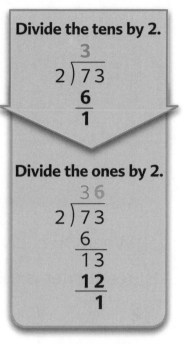

Divide the tens by 2.

$$2\overline{)73} \quad \begin{array}{r} 3 \\ 6 \\ \hline 1 \end{array}$$

Divide the ones by 2.

$$2\overline{)73} \quad \begin{array}{r} 36 \\ 6 \\ \hline 13 \\ 12 \\ \hline 1 \end{array}$$

$$\begin{array}{r} 36\,R\,1 \\ 2\overline{)73} \\ 6 \\ \hline 13 \\ 12 \\ \hline 1 \end{array}$$

When 73 is divided by 2, the quotient is $\boxed{}$

and the remainder is $\boxed{}$.

6.

> Numbers in which the ones digit is **0, 2, 4, 6** or **8** are called **even numbers**.
> Numbers in which the ones digit is **1, 3, 5, 7** or **9** are called **odd numbers**.

What can you say about the remainder in each of the following?

(a) an even number divided by 2
(b) an odd number divided by 2

Exercise 13, pages 98-99

7. $96 \div 4 =$ ⬜

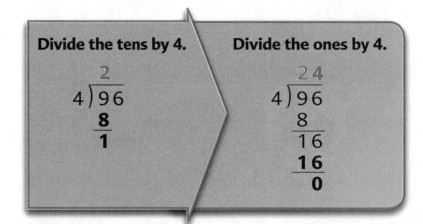

Divide the tens by 4.

```
  2
4)96
  8
  1
```

Divide the ones by 4.

```
  24
4)96
  8
  16
  16
   0
```

When 96 is divided by 4, the quotient is ⬜ and the remainder is ⬜.

8. $80 \div 3 =$ ⬜

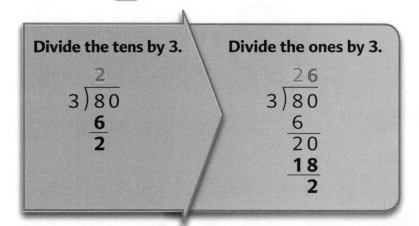

Divide the tens by 3.

```
  2
3)80
  6
  2
```

Divide the ones by 3.

```
  26
3)80
  6
  20
  18
   2
```

When 80 is divided by 3, the quotient is ⬜ and the remainder is ⬜.

9. Find the quotient and remainder for each of the following:
   (a) $48 \div 2$ (b) $60 \div 3$ (c) $54 \div 3$
   (d) $51 \div 4$ (e) $75 \div 5$ (f) $67 \div 5$
   (g) $82 \div 2$ (h) $58 \div 3$ (i) $76 \div 1$
   (j) $80 \div 5$ (k) $91 \div 4$ (l) $60 \div 4$

10. David has 74 wheels.
If he uses 4 wheels to make a toy car, how many toy cars
can he make?

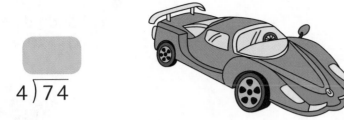

He can make ⬜ toy cars.

⬜ wheels are left over.

11. Justine has 89 yd of wire.
She cuts it into shorter pieces.
Each piece is 3 yd long.
How many pieces can she get?
How long is the piece left over?

She can get ⬜ pieces.

The left over piece is ⬜ yd long.

Exercise 14, pages 100-101

5 Dividing Hundreds, Tens and Ones

$$400 \div 2 = \boxed{}$$

4 hundreds ÷ 2

$$500 \div 2 = \boxed{}$$

5 hundreds ÷ 2

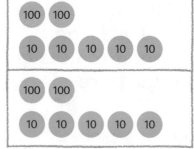

$$550 \div 2 = \boxed{}$$

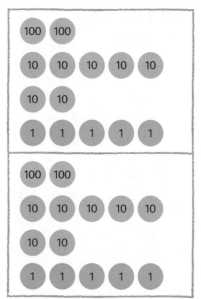

$2\overline{)550}$

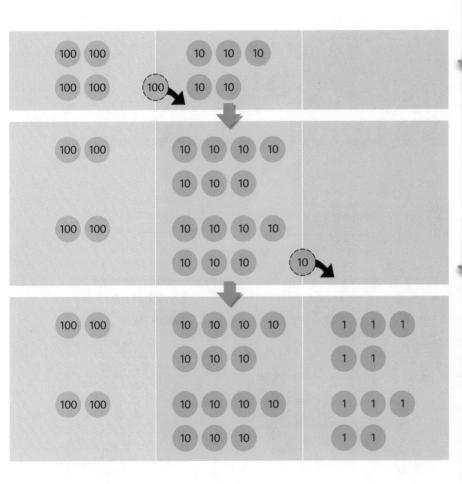

Divide the hundreds by 2.

$$2\overline{)550}$$
$$\underline{4}$$
$$1$$

Divide the tens by 2.

$$2\overline{)550}$$
$$\underline{4}$$
$$15$$
$$\underline{14}$$
$$1$$

Divide the ones by 2.

$$2\overline{)550}$$
$$\underline{4}$$
$$15$$
$$\underline{14}$$
$$10$$
$$\underline{10}$$
$$0$$

1. $426 \div 3 =$ ⬜

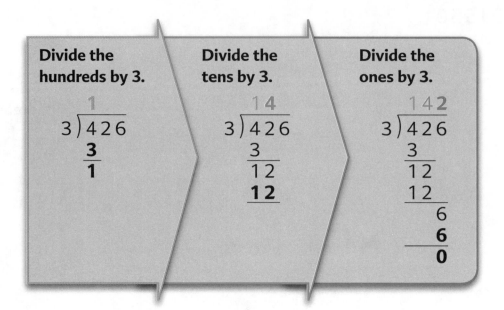

Divide the hundreds by 3.	Divide the tens by 3.	Divide the ones by 3.

```
   1              14             142
3)426          3)426          3)426
  3              3              3
  1              12             12
                 12             12
                                 6
                                 6
                                 0
```

2. $823 \div 4 =$ ⬜

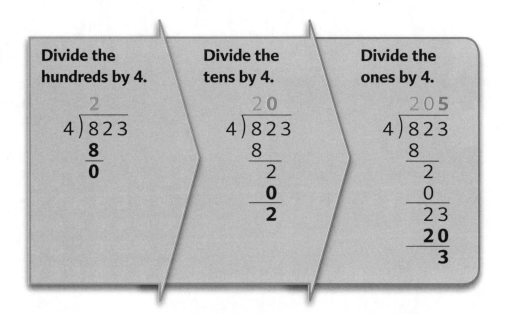

Divide the hundreds by 4.	Divide the tens by 4.	Divide the ones by 4.

```
   2              20             205
4)823          4)823          4)823
  8              8              8
  0              2              2
                 0              0
                 2              23
                                20
                                 3
```

3. Find the quotient and remainder for each of the following:

    (a) $352 \div 4$ (b) $640 \div 2$ (c) $433 \div 5$

    (d) $700 \div 3$ (e) $290 \div 4$ (f) $105 \div 3$

    (g) $249 \div 4$ (h) $374 \div 2$ (i) $511 \div 5$

4. Ashley made 207 muffins.
   She put them into boxes of 4 each.
   How many boxes of muffins were there?
   How many muffins were left over?

   There were ⬜ boxes of muffins.

   ⬜ muffins were left over.

5. 5 packets of ground coffee weigh 750 g.
   How much does each packet weigh?

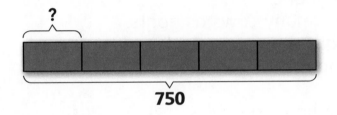

   Each packet weighs ⬜ g.

6. A man has 317 oranges.
   He puts 3 oranges in a bag.
   How many bags of oranges can he make?
   How many oranges will be left over?

   He can make ⬜ bags of oranges.

   ⬜ oranges will be left over.

Exercise 15, pages 102-103

Find the value of each of the following:

	(a)	(b)	(c)	(d)
1.	20 × 5	42 ÷ 2	4 × 51	75 ÷ 3
2.	37 × 3	50 ÷ 5	2 × 78	60 ÷ 5
3.	312 × 4	123 ÷ 3	5 × 500	408 ÷ 4
4.	691 × 5	270 ÷ 4	3 × 607	500 ÷ 3
5.	768 × 3	679 ÷ 5	5 × 705	328 ÷ 5
6.	37 ÷ 3	47 ÷ 3	330 ÷ 4	501 ÷ 3
7.	745 ÷ 5	900 ÷ 4	413 ÷ 3	123 ÷ 4

8. A farmer keeps 64 goats.
   He keeps 5 times as many cows as goats.
   (a) About how many cows does he keep?
   (b) Exactly how many cows does he keep?

9. Mary babysits for 4 hours a day.
   (a) How many hours does she babysit in 26 days?
   (b) If she is paid $3 an hour, how much money does she earn in 26 days?

10. 5 boys share 150 Malaysian stamps and 200 Indonesian stamps equally.
    How many stamps of each country does each boy get?

11. Steve packed 215 oranges into bags of 5 each.
    He sold all the oranges at $2 a bag.
    How much money did he receive?

12. David wants to buy 4 basketballs.
    He has only $55.
    How much more money does he need?

$18 each

1. Find the missing numbers.

   (a) $4243 = 4000 + 200 + 40 +$ ▢

   (b) $4907 -$ ▢ $= 4007$

2. Write the underlined words in numbers.

   (a) The height of Mount Fuji in Japan is <u>three thousand, seven hundred seventy-six</u> meters.

   (b) Mr. Ward bought a computer for <u>two thousand, sixty</u> dollars.

3. Find the value of

   (a) $262 + 138$

   (b) $800 - 236$

4. What does each digit in 5629 stand for?

5. Complete the following regular number patterns.

   (a) 5760, 5770, ▢, 5790

   (b) 4800, 4900, ▢, 5100

   (c) 3040, ▢, 5040, 6040

   (d) 3, 6, ▢, ▢, ▢, 18, ▢

   (e) 45, 40, ▢, ▢, ▢, 20, ▢

6. Replace each ⬤ with **>**, **<**, or **=**.

(a) 4×7 ⬤ $24 + 7$ (b) 4395×0 ⬤ $0 \div 5$

(c) 345×1 ⬤ 1×354 (d) 4×35 ⬤ 35×5

(e) $105 \div 5$ ⬤ 21×5 (f) $4562 + 1438$ ⬤ 1200×4

7. Write **+**, **−**, **×**, or **÷** in place of each ⬤.

(a) 28 ⬤ $4 = 7$ (b) 45 ⬤ $5 = 40$

(c) 36 ⬤ $3 = 108$ (d) 82 ⬤ $2 = 41$

(e) 10 ⬤ $0 = 10$ (f) 600 ⬤ $3 = 1800$

8. Estimate the value of

(a) $6934 - 398$ (b) $4982 + 1298$
(c) 378×4 (d) 3×973

Find the value of each of the following:

	(a)	(b)	(c)
9.	$1672 + 298$	$3984 + 1479$	$804 + 9196$
10.	$3941 - 296$	$4732 - 2415$	$5000 - 4999$
11.	47×3	207×5	789×4
12.	$78 \div 3$	$700 \div 4$	$451 \div 5$

13. 1628 boys and 1092 girls took part in an art competition. How many children took part altogether?

14. There were 4525 concert tickets for sale in the morning.
    1909 tickets were sold at the end of the day.
    How many tickets were left?

15. There were 485 gal of gas in 1 drum.
    (a) About how many gallons of gas were there in
         4 such drums?
    (b) Exactly how many gallons of gas were there in
         4 such drums?

16. (a) A tailor bought 563 yd of cloth to make dresses.
         He used 3 yd to make each dress.
         How many dresses did he make?
         How many yards of cloth were left?

    (b) If he sold all the dresses at $5 each,
         how much money did he receive?

17. There were 1052 books in a children's library.
    650 of them were checked out.
    226 of the books left were picture books.
    How many chapter books were left?

18. Kylie has $240.
    Nicole has 3 times as much money as Kylie.
    How much money do they have altogether?

4 MULTIPLICATION TABLES OF 6, 7, 8 AND 9

1 Multiplying and Dividing by 6

1 × 1	1 × 2	1 × 3	1 × 4	1 × 5
2 × 1	2 × 2	2 × 3	2 × 4	2 × 5
3 × 1	3 × 2	3 × 3	3 × 4	3 × 5
4 × 1	4 × 2	4 × 3	4 × 4	4 × 5
5 × 1	5 × 2	5 × 3	5 × 4	5 × 5
6 × 1	6 × 2	6 × 3	6 × 4	6 × 5
7 × 1	7 × 2	7 × 3	7 × 4	7 × 5
8 × 1	8 × 2	8 × 3	8 × 4	8 × 5
9 × 1	9 × 2	9 × 3	9 × 4	9 × 5
10 × 1	10 × 2	10 × 3	10 × 4	10 × 5

1 × 6	1 × 7	1 × 8	1 × 9	1 × 10
2 × 6	2 × 7	2 × 8	2 × 9	2 × 10
3 × 6	3 × 7	3 × 8	3 × 9	3 × 10
4 × 6	4 × 7	4 × 8	4 × 9	4 × 10
5 × 6	5 × 7	5 × 8	5 × 9	5 × 10
6 × 6	6 × 7	6 × 8	6 × 9	6 × 10
7 × 6	7 × 7	7 × 8	7 × 9	7 × 10
8 × 6	8 × 7	8 × 8	8 × 9	8 × 10
9 × 6	9 × 7	9 × 8	9 × 9	9 × 10
10 × 6	10 × 7	10 × 8	10 × 9	10 × 10

Do you know the answers of all the cards?

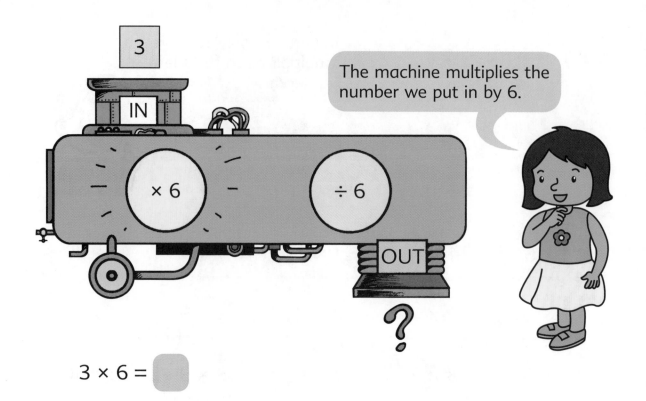

The machine multiplies the number we put in by 6.

$3 \times 6 =$

The machine divides the number we put in by 6.

$30 \div 6 =$

1. (a)

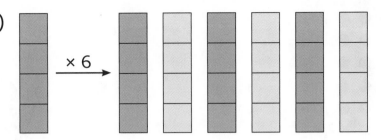

$$4 \times 6 = \boxed{}$$

(b)

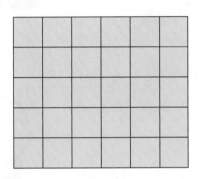

$5 \times 6 = 6 \times 5$

$$5 \times 6 = \boxed{}$$

$$6 \times 5 = \boxed{}$$

2. (a)

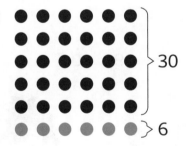

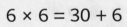 30

6

$6 \times 6 = 30 + 6$

$$6 \times 5 = 30$$

$$6 \times 6 = \boxed{}$$

(b)

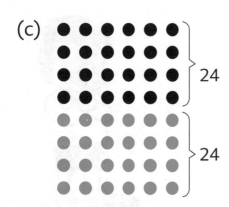

> 30

> 12

$6 \times 5 = 30$

$6 \times 2 = 12$

$6 \times 7 = $

$6 \times 7 = 30 + 12$

(c)

> 24

> 24

$6 \times 4 = 24$

$6 \times 8 = $

$6 \times 8 = 24 \times 2$

(d)

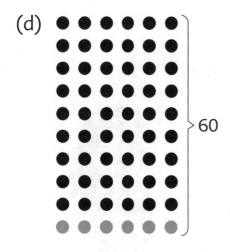

> 60

$6 \times 10 = 60$

$6 \times 9 \ = $

$6 \times 9 = 60 - 6$

3. Complete the number sentences.

$1 \times 6 = 6$ $6 \times 1 =$

$2 \times 6 = 12$ $6 \times 2 =$

$3 \times 6 = 18$ $6 \times 3 =$

$4 \times 6 = 24$ $6 \times 4 =$

$5 \times 6 = 30$ $6 \times 5 =$

$6 \times 6 =$ $6 \times 6 =$

$7 \times 6 =$ $6 \times 7 =$

$8 \times 6 =$ $6 \times 8 =$

$9 \times 6 =$ $6 \times 9 =$

$10 \times 6 = 60$ $6 \times 10 =$

Exercise 1, pages 111-112

4.

$\boxed{} \times 6 = 30$
$6 \times \boxed{} = 30$ — $30 \div 6 = \boxed{}$

$\boxed{} \times 6 = 42$
$6 \times \boxed{} = 42$ — $42 \div 6 = \boxed{}$

$\boxed{} \times 6 = 48$
$6 \times \boxed{} = 48$ — $48 \div 6 = \boxed{}$

$\boxed{} \times 6 = 54$
$6 \times \boxed{} = 54$ — $54 \div 6 = \boxed{}$

Exercise 2, pages 113-114

5. (a) Estimate the product of 285 and 6.

$$300 \times 6 = \boxed{}$$

285 is 300 when rounded to the nearest 100.

Check the actual product with the estimate. Is it close?

(b) Multiply 285 by 6.

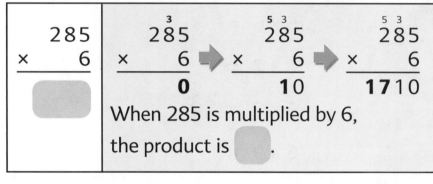

| $\begin{array}{r} 285 \\ \times\ \ \ \ 6 \\ \hline \boxed{} \end{array}$ | $\begin{array}{r} \overset{3}{2}85 \\ \times\ \ \ \ 6 \\ \hline 0 \end{array}$ ➡ $\begin{array}{r} \overset{5\ 3}{2}85 \\ \times\ \ \ \ 6 \\ \hline 10 \end{array}$ ➡ $\begin{array}{r} \overset{5\ 3}{2}85 \\ \times\ \ \ \ 6 \\ \hline 1710 \end{array}$ |

When 285 is multiplied by 6, the product is $\boxed{}$.

6. Find the product of each of the following.
Use estimation to see if your answer is reasonable.
   (a) 34 and 6   (b) 57 and 6   (c) 6 and 69
   (d) 108 and 6   (e) 472 and 6   (f) 6 and 910

Exercise 3, pages 115-116

7. Divide 325 by 6.

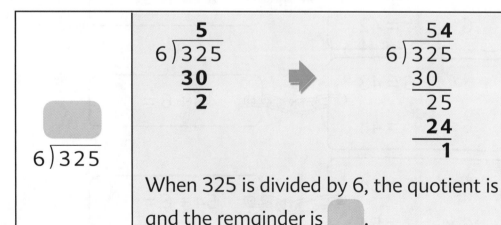

$$6\overline{)325}$$

$$\begin{array}{r} 5 \\ 6\overline{)325} \\ 30 \\ \hline 2 \end{array}$$

➡

$$\begin{array}{r} 54 \\ 6\overline{)325} \\ 30 \\ \hline 25 \\ 24 \\ \hline 1 \end{array}$$

When 325 is divided by 6, the quotient is $\boxed{}$ and the remainder is $\boxed{}$.

8. Divide 8492 by 6.

$$6\overline{)8492}$$

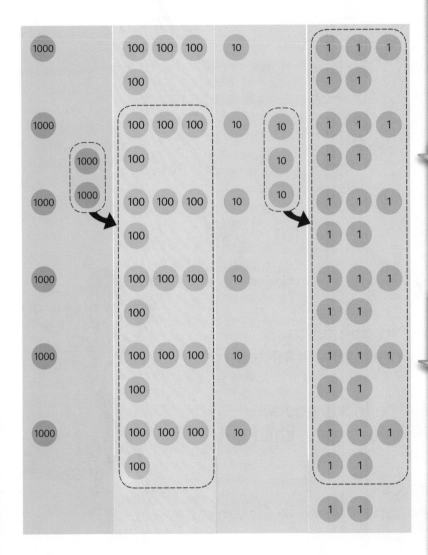

Divide the thousands by 6.

$$
\begin{array}{r}
1 \\
6\overline{)8492} \\
\underline{6} \\
2
\end{array}
$$

Divide the hundreds by 6.

$$
\begin{array}{r}
14 \\
6\overline{)8492} \\
\underline{6} \\
24 \\
\underline{24} \\
0
\end{array}
$$

Divide the tens by 6.

$$
\begin{array}{r}
141 \\
6\overline{)8492} \\
\underline{6} \\
24 \\
\underline{24} \\
09 \\
\underline{6} \\
3
\end{array}
$$

Divide the ones by 6.

$$
\begin{array}{r}
1415 \\
6\overline{)8492} \\
\underline{6} \\
24 \\
\underline{24} \\
09 \\
\underline{6} \\
32 \\
\underline{30} \\
2
\end{array}
$$

9. Find the quotient and remainder for each of the following:

   (a) 96 ÷ 6   (b) 89 ÷ 6   (c) 75 ÷ 6
   (d) 342 ÷ 6   (e) 708 ÷ 6   (f) 615 ÷ 6
   (g) 9804 ÷ 6   (h) 4632 ÷ 6   (i) 1098 ÷ 6

Exercise 4, pages 117-118

Find the value of each of the following:

	(a)	(b)	(c)
1.	6 × 3	6 × 4	7 × 6
2.	18 ÷ 6	24 ÷ 6	42 ÷ 6
3.	43 × 6	94 × 6	6 × 57
4.	80 ÷ 6	405 ÷ 6	562 ÷ 6
5.	318 × 6	189 × 6	504 × 6
6.	2817 ÷ 6	6848 ÷ 6	7567 ÷ 6

7. Find the missing numbers.

(a) 6 × ☐ = 36   (b) ☐ × 4 = 24

(c) 7 × ☐ = 42   (d) ☐ × 6 = 60

8. There are 6 players in one team.
   How many players are there in 14 teams?

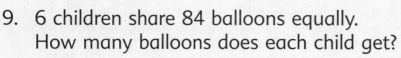

9. 6 children share 84 balloons equally.
   How many balloons does each child get?

10. John earns $85 a week.
    How much money can he earn in 6 weeks?

11. Mr. Kim tied 192 books into bundles of 6 each.
    How many bundles were there?

12. Mrs. Larson bought 6 m of cloth for $84.
    Find the cost of 5 m of cloth.

Exercise 5, pages 119-121

2 Multiplying and Dividing by 7

Sam made this table to help him collect money.

Number of cakes	1	2	3	4	5
Price	$7	$14	$21	$28	$35

(a) Amy bought 2 cakes.
How much did she pay?

(b) Mrs. Lee ordered 4 cakes for a party.
How much did she pay?

(c) Sara paid Sam $35.
How many cakes did Sam sell her?

(d) How many cakes could Ryan buy with $42?

1. (a)

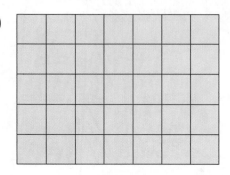

$3 \times 7 =$

(b)

$5 \times 7 =$

$7 \times 5 =$

2. (a)

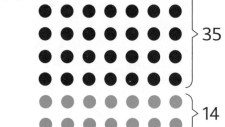

35

7

$7 \times 6 = 35 + 7$

$7 \times 5 = 35$

$7 \times 6 =$

(b)

35

14

$7 \times 7 = 35 + 14$

$7 \times 5 = 35$

$7 \times 2 = 14$

$7 \times 7 =$

(c)

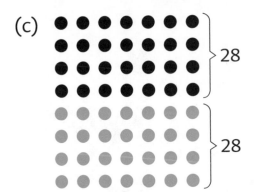

} 28

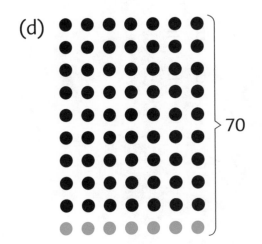

} 28

$7 \times 4 = 28$

$7 \times 8 = $

(d)

$7 \times 9 = 70 - 7$

} 70

$7 \times 10 = 70$

$7 \times 9 \ = $

3.

October						
Sun	Mon	Tue	Wed	Thu	Fri	Sat
1	2	3	4	5	6	7
8	9	10	11	12	13	14
15	16	17	18	19	20	21
22	23	24	25	26	27	28
29	30	31				

There are 7 days in a week.

There are ___ days in 2 weeks.

There are ___ days in 4 weeks.

There are ___ days in 10 weeks.

4. Complete the number sentences.

$1 \times 7 = 7$ $7 \times 1 =$ ☐

$2 \times 7 = 14$ $7 \times 2 =$ ☐

$3 \times 7 = 21$ $7 \times 3 =$ ☐

$4 \times 7 =$ ☐ $7 \times 4 =$ ☐

$5 \times 7 =$ ☐ $7 \times 5 =$ ☐

$6 \times 7 =$ ☐ $7 \times 6 =$ ☐

$7 \times 7 =$ ☐ $7 \times 7 =$ ☐

$8 \times 7 =$ ☐ $7 \times 8 =$ ☐

$9 \times 7 =$ ☐ $7 \times 9 =$ ☐

$10 \times 7 =$ ☐ $7 \times 10 =$ ☐

5. Find the value of
   (a) 6×7 (b) 7×7 (c) 7×9
   (d) $56 \div 7$ (e) $70 \div 7$ (f) $21 \div 7$

Exercise 6, pages 122-124

6. (a) Estimate the product of 867 and 7.

   ☐ $\times 7 =$ ☐

   The product of 867×7 is about ☐.

Round 867 to the nearest hundred.

(b) Find the product of 867 and 7.

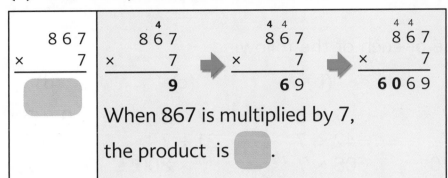

$$
\begin{array}{r}
867 \\
\times \quad 7 \\
\hline

\end{array}
$$

$$
\begin{array}{r}
\overset{4}{8}67 \\
\times \quad 7 \\
\hline
9
\end{array}
$$
⮕
$$
\begin{array}{r}
\overset{4}{8}\overset{4}{6}7 \\
\times \quad 7 \\
\hline
69
\end{array}
$$
⮕
$$
\begin{array}{r}
\overset{4}{8}\overset{4}{6}7 \\
\times \quad 7 \\
\hline
6069
\end{array}
$$

When 867 is multiplied by 7,

the product is ▢.

Check the actual product with the estimate. Is it close?

7. Multiply.
   (a) 56 × 7   (b) 63 × 7   (c) 7 × 71
   (d) 920 × 7   (e) 804 × 7   (f) 7 × 218

Exercise 7, pages 125-126

8. Divide 7982 by 7.

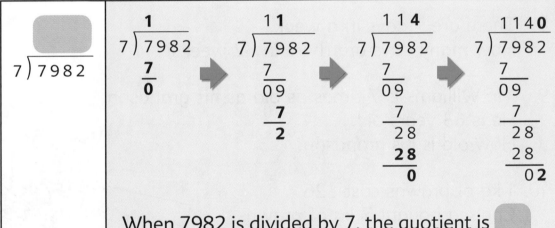

$$
7\overline{)7982}
$$

$$
\begin{array}{r}
1 \\
7\overline{)7982} \\
7 \\
\hline
0
\end{array}
$$
⮕
$$
\begin{array}{r}
11 \\
7\overline{)7982} \\
7 \\
\hline
09 \\
7 \\
\hline
2
\end{array}
$$
⮕
$$
\begin{array}{r}
114 \\
7\overline{)7982} \\
7 \\
\hline
09 \\
7 \\
\hline
28 \\
28 \\
\hline
0
\end{array}
$$
⮕
$$
\begin{array}{r}
1140 \\
7\overline{)7982} \\
7 \\
\hline
09 \\
7 \\
\hline
28 \\
28 \\
\hline
02
\end{array}
$$

When 7982 is divided by 7, the quotient is ▢

and the remainder is ▢.

9. Divide.
   (a) 75 ÷ 7   (b) 84 ÷ 7   (c) 64 ÷ 7
   (d) 91 ÷ 7   (e) 98 ÷ 7   (f) 80 ÷ 7

10. Divide.
    (a)   108 ÷ 7   (b)   231 ÷ 7   (c)   682 ÷ 7
    (d) 7306 ÷ 7   (e) 9549 ÷ 7   (f) 7050 ÷ 7

Exercise 8, pages 127-128

PRACTICE B

Find the value of each of the following:

	(a)	(b)	(c)	(d)
1.	4 × 7	7 × 6	7 × 3	9 × 7
2.	28 ÷ 7	42 ÷ 7	21 ÷ 7	63 ÷ 7
3.	7 × 40	608 × 7	7 × 800	930 × 7
4.	95 ÷ 7	540 ÷ 7	714 ÷ 7	805 ÷ 7
5.	214 × 7	342 × 7	765 × 7	986 × 7
6.	8373 ÷ 7	5563 ÷ 7	9055 ÷ 7	6746 ÷ 7

7. A baker needs 7 eggs to bake a cake.
   He has 150 eggs.
   How many cakes can he bake?
   How many eggs will be left over?

8. There are 7 days in a week.
   How many days are there in 52 weeks?

9. Mr. Williams is 7 times as old as his grandson.
   He is 63 years old.
   How old is his grandson?

10. 1 kg of prawns cost $26.
    Chelsea bought 7 kg of prawns.
    How much did she pay?

$26 for 1 kg

11. Lindsey spent $84 on 7 towels.
    What was the cost of 1 towel?

12. Taylor packed 112 lemons into bags of 7 each.
    She sold all the lemons at $3 a bag.
    How much money did she receive?

Exercise 9, pages 129-131

Find the value of each of the following:

	(a)	(b)	(c)	(d)
1.	6 × 6	7 × 8	6 × 10	7 × 7
2.	36 ÷ 6	42 ÷ 6	60 ÷ 6	49 ÷ 7
3.	67 × 7	0 × 7	10 × 1	513 × 7
4.	304 ÷ 6	0 ÷ 7	10 ÷ 10	847 ÷ 7

5. Emily has a rope 161 in. long.
   She cuts it into 7 equal pieces.
   What is the length of each piece?

6. Mr. Jefferson bought 28 kg of pineapples.
   How much did he spend?

$6 for 1 kg

7. A baker bought 84 eggs to bake cakes.
   He used 6 eggs to bake each cake.
   How many cakes did he bake?

8. 6 children shared 3 boxes of toy soldiers equally.
   Each box contained 48 toy soldiers.
   How many toy soldiers did each child get?

9. There were 7 boxes of blue pens and red pens.
   There were 12 pens in each box.
   If there were 36 red pens, how many blue pens were there?

10. Wendy bought 35 m of cloth at $6 for 1 m.
    She still had $25 left after paying for the cloth.
    How much did she have at first?

❸ Multiplying and Dividing by 8

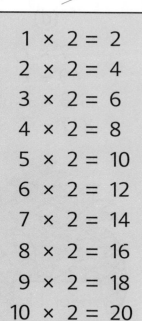

×2   ×2

1 × 2 = 2	1 × 4 = 4	1 × 8 = 8
2 × 2 = 4	2 × 4 = 8	2 × 8 = 16
3 × 2 = 6	3 × 4 = 12	3 × 8 = 24
4 × 2 = 8	4 × 4 = 16	4 × 8 = 32
5 × 2 = 10	5 × 4 = 20	5 × 8 = 40
6 × 2 = 12	6 × 4 = 24	6 × 8 = 48
7 × 2 = 14	7 × 4 = 28	7 × 8 = 56
8 × 2 = 16	8 × 4 = 32	8 × 8 = ?
9 × 2 = 18	9 × 4 = 36	9 × 8 = ?
10 × 2 = 20	10 × 4 = 40	10 × 8 = 80

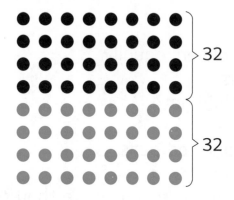

32

32

8 × 4 = 32

8 × 8 =

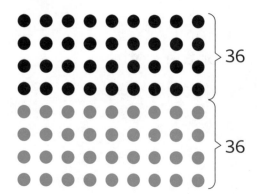

36

36

9 × 4 = 36

9 × 8 =

1. An octopus has 8 arms.

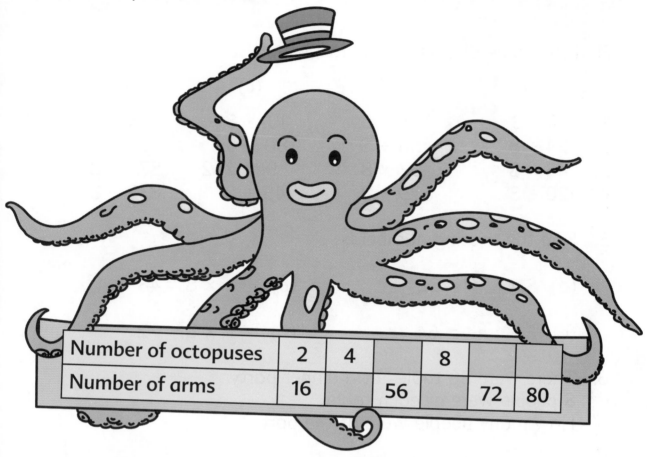

Number of octopuses	2	4		8		
Number of arms	16		56		72	80

2. Multiply.
   (a) 3 × 8   (b) 5 × 8   (c) 8 × 8
   (d) 8 × 4   (e) 8 × 7   (f) 8 × 9

3. Divide.
   (a) 80 ÷ 8   (b) 48 ÷ 8   (c) 24 ÷ 8
   (d) 72 ÷ 8   (e) 56 ÷ 8   (f) 40 ÷ 8

Exercise 10, pages 132-133

4. Multiply.
   (a)   56 × 8   (b)   79 × 8   (c) 8 × 68
   (d) 418 × 8   (e) 305 × 8   (f) 8 × 620

Exercise 11, pages 134-135

5. Divide.
   (a)   98 ÷ 8   (b) 112 ÷ 8   (c) 807 ÷ 8
   (d) 305 ÷ 8   (e) 664 ÷ 8   (f) 960 ÷ 8

Exercise 12, pages 136-137

Find the value of each of the following:

	(a)	(b)	(c)	(d)
1.	8 × 3	6 × 8	10 × 8	8 × 8
2.	24 ÷ 8	56 ÷ 8	80 ÷ 8	64 ÷ 8
3.	43 × 8	97 × 8	8 × 262	874 × 8
4.	120 ÷ 8	579 ÷ 8	745 ÷ 8	832 ÷ 8

5. Find the missing numbers.

   (a) 8 × ⬚ = 32   (b) ⬚ × 8 = 48

   (c) 8 × ⬚ = 64   (d) ⬚ × 8 = 72

6. There were 36 tables at a dinner party.
   8 people were at each table.
   How many people were at the party?

7. A bucket holds 18 liters.
   8 buckets of water can fill a tank.
   How many liters of water does the tank hold?

8. Kathy baked 390 tarts.
   She put them into boxes of 8 each.
   How many boxes did she have?
   How many tarts were left over?

9. A gardener bought 12 watering cans.
   Each can cost $8.
   If he gave the cashier $100, how much change did
   he receive?

Exercise 13, pages 138-140

Find the value of each of the following:

	(a)	(b)	(c)	(d)
1.	6 × 7	7 × 8	8 × 10	8 × 9
2.	42 ÷ 6	56 ÷ 7	48 ÷ 8	72 ÷ 8
3.	73 ÷ 7	1 × 8	0 × 8	150 ÷ 8
4.	943 ÷ 8	8 ÷ 1	0 ÷ 8	872 ÷ 6

5. A grocer had 145 kg of sugar.
    He packed the sugar into bags of 6 kg each.
    How many bags were there?
    How many kilograms of sugar were left over?

6. Mrs. Sanchez wants to buy umbrellas.
    Each umbrella costs $7.
    How many umbrellas can she buy
    with $168?

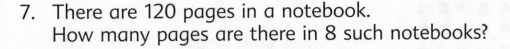

$7
each

7. There are 120 pages in a notebook.
    How many pages are there in 8 such notebooks?

8. Tony wants to buy 6 chairs which cost $28 each.
    He has only $100.
    How much more money does he need?

9. 8 people went to the seaside.
    They rented a boat for 6 hours.
    If they shared the cost equally,
    how much did each person spend?

BOATS
for hire
$12 for 1 hour

4 Multiplying and Dividing by 9

1 × 10 = 10	1 × 9 = 9	10 − 1
2 × 10 = 20	2 × 9 = 18	20 − 2
3 × 10 = 30	3 × 9 = 27	30 − 3
4 × 10 = 40	4 × 9 = 36	40 − 4
5 × 10 = 50	5 × 9 = 45	50 − 5
6 × 10 = 60	6 × 9 = 54	60 − 6
7 × 10 = 70	7 × 9 = 63	70 − 7
8 × 10 = 80	8 × 9 = ?	80 − 8
9 × 10 = 90	9 × 9 = ?	90 − 9
10 × 10 = 100	10 × 9 = 90	100 − 10

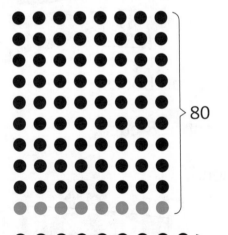

80

$8 \times 10 = 80$

$8 \times 9 \ =$

90

$9 \times 10 = 90$

$9 \times 9 \ =$

1. Add the tens digit and ones digit of each product.

   The answer is [ ].

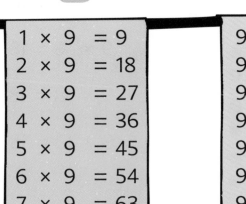

1 × 9	= 9		9 × 1	= 9
2 × 9	= 18		9 × 2	= 18
3 × 9	= 27		9 × 3	= 27
4 × 9	= 36		9 × 4	= 36
5 × 9	= 45		9 × 5	= 45
6 × 9	= 54		9 × 6	= 54
7 × 9	= 63		9 × 7	= 63
8 × 9	= 72		9 × 8	= 72
9 × 9	= 81		9 × 9	= 81
10 × 9	= 90		9 × 10	= 90

2. Here is an interesting way to multiply by 9.

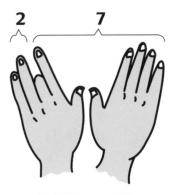

3 × 9 = 27

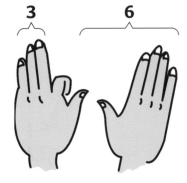

4 × 9 = 36

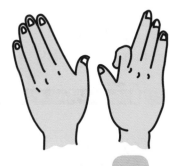

7 × 9 = [ ]

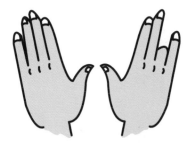

9 × 9 = [ ]

3. (a)

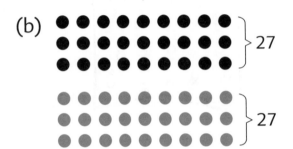

$$9 \times 2 = 18$$

$$9 \times 4 = 18 \times \boxed{}$$

$$9 \times 6 = 18 \times \boxed{}$$

$$9 \times 8 = 18 \times \boxed{}$$

$$9 \times 10 = 18 \times \boxed{}$$

(b)

$$9 \times 3 = 27$$

$$9 \times 6 = 27 \times \boxed{}$$

4. Multiply.

   (a) 2×9 (b) 4×9 (c) 9×3
   (d) 8×9 (e) 9×9 (f) 9×7

5. Divide.

   (a) $90 \div 9$ (b) $63 \div 9$ (c) $45 \div 9$
   (d) $54 \div 9$ (e) $72 \div 9$ (f) $81 \div 9$

Exercise 14, pages 141-142

6. Multiply.

   (a) 54×9 (b) 73×9 (c) 9×80
   (d) 201×9 (e) 678×9 (f) 9×609

Exercise 15, pages 143-144

7. Divide.

   (a) $97 \div 9$ (b) $108 \div 9$ (c) $89 \div 9$
   (d) $620 \div 9$ (e) $903 \div 9$ (f) $145 \div 9$

Exercise 16, pages 145-146

Find the value of each of the following:

	(a)	(b)	(c)	(d)
1.	3 × 9	9 × 4	9 × 5	9 × 9
2.	27 ÷ 9	36 ÷ 9	45 ÷ 9	81 ÷ 9
3.	36 × 9	9 × 400	657 × 9	198 × 9
4.	954 ÷ 9	563 ÷ 9	790 ÷ 9	823 ÷ 9

5. Mary bought 9 pieces of string, each 18 m long.
   How many meters of string did she buy?

6. 25 boys went camping.
   Each boy brought 9 cans of food.
   How many cans did they bring altogether?

7. Tyrone bought 9 T-shirts for $144.
   How much did one T-shirt cost?

8. David cut a wire 918 m long into pieces.
   Each piece was 9 m long.
   How many pieces did he get?

9. Cameron uses 185 liters of gas a month.
   How much gas does he use in 9 months?

10. A tailor bought 9 packets of buttons.
    There were 120 buttons in each packet.
    He used 8 buttons on a dress.
    How many dresses did he make if he used all the buttons?

Exercise 17, pages 147-149

Find the value of each of the following:

	(a)	(b)	(c)	(d)
1.	9 × 6	7 × 10	8 × 8	6 × 6
2.	54 ÷ 6	70 ÷ 7	64 ÷ 8	36 ÷ 6
3.	69 × 8	1 × 9	0 × 9	901 × 6
4.	581 ÷ 9	9 ÷ 1	0 ÷ 9	749 ÷ 7

5. Mrs. Washington gives each of her children $7.

   If she gives a total of $28 to her children, how many children does she have?

6. A tank holds 126 liters.
   A bucket holds 9 liters.
   How many buckets of water will fill up the tank?

7. Matthew worked for 7 days.
   He was paid $36 each day.
   How much money did he receive?

8. There are 136 roses.
   There are 6 times as many sunflowers as roses.
   How many sunflowers are there?

9. Eric had 112 tomatoes.
   8 of them were rotten.
   He packed the good tomatoes into packets of 8 each.
   How many packets of tomatoes did he get?

⑤ More Multiplication and Division

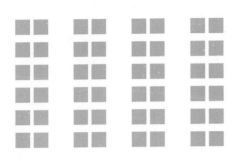

$6 \times 2 \times 4 = 12 \times$ ◻

$6 \times 2 \times 4 =$ ◻

$6 \times 4 \times 2 = 24 \times$ ◻

$6 \times 4 \times 2 =$ ◻

$4 \times 2 \times 6 =$ ◻

$2 \times 4 \times 6 =$ ◻

1. $7 \times 5 =$ ◻ $7 \times 5 \times 3 =$ ◻

$7 \times 3 =$ ◻ $7 \times 3 \times 5 =$ ◻

$5 \times 3 =$ ◻ $5 \times 3 \times 7 =$ ◻

$5 \times 7 =$ ◻ $5 \times 7 \times 3 =$ ◻

$2 \times 3 =$ ◻ $2 \times 3 \times 7 =$ ◻

$2 \times 7 =$ ◻ $2 \times 7 \times 3 =$ ◻

2. (a) Find the value of 50 × 7 × 2.

$$50 \times 7 \times 2 = 50 \times 2 \times 7$$

$$100 \times 7 = \boxed{}$$

$$50 \times 7 \times 2 = \boxed{}$$

I can solve this by first finding the product of 50 and 2. Then it is easy to solve 100 × 7.

(b) Find the value of 24 × 9 × 10.

$$24 \times 9 \times 10 = \boxed{}$$

3. (a) $9 \times 5 \times 8 = 8 \times 5 \times \boxed{}$

(b) $45 \times 12 \times 6 = 6 \times \boxed{} \times 45$

4. If 39 × 23 × 6 = 5382, what is the value of 6 × 23 × 39?

5. Find the missing numbers.

(a) $9 \times 8 \times 3 = \boxed{} \times 3 \times 8$ (b) $7 \times 11 \times 12 = 12 \times \boxed{} \times 7$

(c) $9 \times 6 = 3 \times \boxed{} \times 6$ (d) $8 \times 5 \times 4 = \boxed{} \times 20$

(e) $3 \times 6 \times 8 = 48 \times \boxed{}$ (f) $25 \times 38 \times 4 = 100 \times \boxed{}$

Exercise 18, pages 150-151

6. (a) $6 \div 3 = \boxed{}$

    (1)(1)   (1)(1)   (1)(1)

    6 ones ÷ 3 = $\boxed{}$ ones

   (b) $60 \div 3 = \boxed{}$

    (10)(10)   (10)(10)   (10)(10)

    6 tens ÷ 3 = $\boxed{}$ tens

   (c) $600 \div 3 = \boxed{}$

    (100)(100)   (100)(100)   (100)(100)

    6 hundreds ÷ 3 = $\boxed{}$ hundreds

   (d) $6000 \div 3 = \boxed{}$

    (1000)(1000)   (1000)(1000)   (1000)(1000)

    6 thousands ÷ 3 = $\boxed{}$ thousands

7. $40 \div 8 = \boxed{}$

   $400 \div 8 = \boxed{}$

   $4000 \div 8 = \boxed{}$

   $40\,00 \div 8 = 5\,00$

8. Divide.
   (a)   9 ÷ 3   (b)   90 ÷ 3   (c)   900 ÷ 3
   (d)   40 ÷ 2   (e)   360 ÷ 6   (f)   400 ÷ 10
   (g) 320 ÷ 8   (h) 2400 ÷ 4   (i)   1000 ÷ 5

Exercise 19, pages 152-153

9. Estimate the value of 167 ÷ 3.

200 ÷ 3 = ?

I can't round to the nearest hundred.
There will be a remainder.

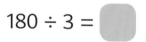

$$167 \begin{cases} \textbf{15}0 \div 3 \\ \textbf{18}0 \div 3 \end{cases}$$

180 ÷ 3 = ☐

The value of 167 ÷ 3 is about ☐.

10. (a) Estimate the value of 4693 ÷ 8.

4693 ÷ 8

8 × 5 = 40
8 × 6 = 48

46 is closer to 48 than 40.

4800 ÷ 8 = ☐

The value of 4693 ÷ 8 is about ☐.

(b) Find the value of 4693 ÷ 8.

Check the actual quotient with the estimate. Is the answer close?

4693 ÷ 8 = ☐

11. Estimate the value of
(a) 843 ÷ 4   (b) 378 ÷ 6   (c) 839 ÷ 9
(d) 9327 ÷ 10   (e) 3982 ÷ 7   (f) 5890 ÷ 8

 Exercise 20, page 154

1. Round each number to the nearest ten.
   (a) 55 (b) 271 (c) 4005 (d) 6999

2. There are 3525 students in a school.
   (a) How many students are there to the nearest hundred?
   (b) How many students are there to the nearest thousand?

3. Peter has about $1500 in the bank.
   Does he have $1551 or $1495 in the bank?

4. Write the numbers.
   (a) five thousand, five hundred five
   (b) nine thousand, one
   (c) one thousand, ninety-nine

5. Arrange these numbers in order, beginning with the smallest.

   | 9591 | 5101 | 995 | 500 | 5050 |

6. Write the numbers in expanded form.
   (a) 1111 (b) 6019 (c) 8910

7. Replace each ⬤ with > or <.

   (a) 875 ⬤ 785

   (b) 909 ⬤ 1001

   (c) 3500 ⬤ 3056

8. How many legs do 9 spiders have, if one spider has 8 legs?

9. Find the value of each of the following:
   (a) 15×1
   (b) 1×99
   (c) 9×0
   (d) 0×7
   (e) $0 \div 9$
   (f) $8 \div 8$

10. Find the product of each of the following.
    Use estimation to see if your answer is reasonable.
    (a) 278×7
    (b) 1173×8
    (c) 678×9

11. Write **+**, **−**, **×**, or **÷** in place of each ⬤.

    (a) 30 ⬤ $5 = 6$
    (b) 5 ⬤ $30 = 35$

    (c) 50 ⬤ $2 = 6 \times 8$
    (d) 9 ⬤ $8 = 8 \times 9$

    (e) 48 ⬤ $8 = 8$ ⬤ 7
    (f) 72 ⬤ $9 = 9$ ⬤ 7

12. Which of the following are true?
    (a) $40 \div 5 > 20 \times 2$
    (b) $1 + 1 = 1 \times 1$
    (c) $0 \times 9 < 2 + 0$
    (d) $32 \div 4 = 2 + 3 + 3$
    (e) $45 - 9 > 35 \times 1$
    (f) $0 \div 6 < 0$

13. Use mental calculation to find the value of each of
    the following.
    (a) $68 + 39$
    (b) $149 + 60$
    (c) $561 + 128$
    (d) $92 - 48$
    (e) $893 - 98$
    (f) $450 - 70$
    (g) 400×8
    (h) 60×7
    (i) 2000×4
    (j) $200 \div 10$
    (k) $3000 \div 6$
    (l) $7200 \div 9$

14. (a) What number is 680 more than 3452?
    (b) 97 is 349 less than what number?
    (c) 480 is how much more than 289?

15. What number goes in the ☐?

(a) $4928 - ☐ = 349$

(b) $81 \div ☐ = 9$

(c) $9 \times 8 \times 10 = 10 \times ☐ \times 9$

(d) $7 \times ☐ \times 4 = 4 \times 42$

16. Find the value of the following.
Use estimation to check if your answers are reasonable.

(a) $489 \div 7$

(b) $8942 \div 6$

(c) $899 \div 9$

17. Mr. Lewis bought 6 lb of halibut.
1 lb of halibut cost $6.
How much did he pay?

18. A jacket costs 7 times as much as a T-shirt.
If the T-shirt costs $26, what is the total cost of the T-shirt and the jacket?

19. Dorothy bought a refrigerator.
She paid $245 in the first month and $103 each month for another 8 months.
What was the cost of the refrigerator?

20. Melissa bought 27 apples at 3 for $2.
How much did she pay in all?

21. There are 8 stamps in a set.
Miguel bought 120 sets of stamps.
After selling some stamps, he had 680 stamps left.
How many stamps did he sell?

5 DATA ANALYSIS

1 Presenting Data

These cards show the names and weights of five children.

Name : Rachel Weight : 38 kg	Name : Veronica Weight : 39 kg

Name : Tasha Weight : 38 kg	Name : Roy Weight : 43 kg	Name : Juan Weight : 40 kg

The data can be presented in the form of a table like this:

Name	Weight
Rachel	38 kg
Veronica	39 kg
Tasha	38 kg
Roy	43 kg
Juan	40 kg

The data can also be presented in a bar graph:

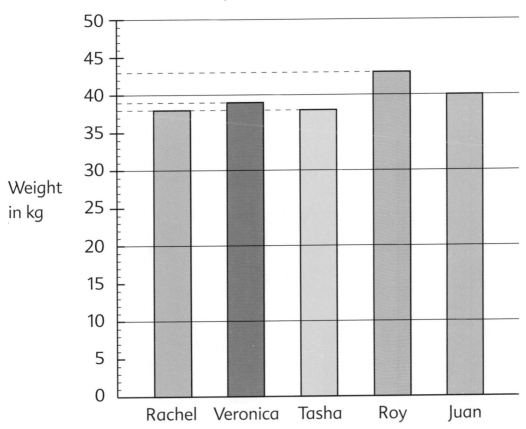

1. This tally chart shows the number of books read by four children in one month.

Name	Number of books
David	~~HHH~~ |||
Pablo	~~HHH~~ ~~HHH~~ ~~HHH~~	
Lauren	~~HHH~~ ~~HHH~~ ||||
Rosa	~~HHH~~ ~~HHH~~

(a) Who read the greatest number of books in one month?

(b) How many more books did Lauren read than David in one month?

(c) Draw a bar graph to show the data given in the chart.

2. The bar graph shows the number of cars sold by Patrick in six months.
   Use the graph to answer the questions which follow.

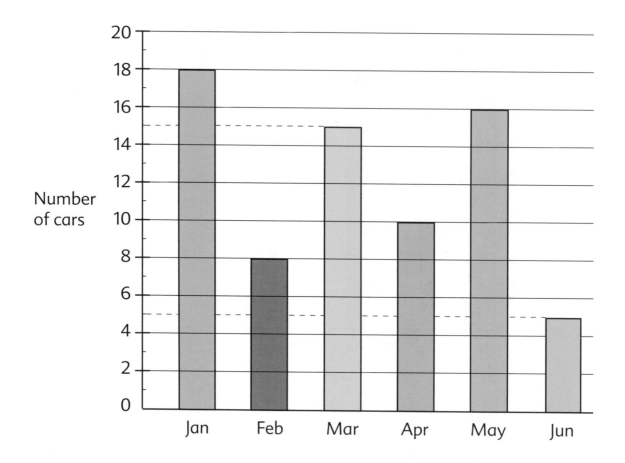

(a) How many cars did Patrick sell in March?

(b) In which months did Patrick sell fewer than 10 cars?

(c) In which month did Patrick sell the greatest number of cars?

(d) How many more cars were sold in May than in April?

(e) In which month were half as many cars sold as in May?

3. Make a table to show the data given in the bar graph above.

Exercise 1, pages 162-166

4. The table shows the number of people who attended four courses in a community center.
Use the table to answer the questions which follow.

Course	Men	Women
Cooking	6	21
Art	14	11
Computer	25	24
Dancing	12	18

(a) How many people attended the cooking course?

(b) How many more women than men attended the dancing course?

(c) How many more people attended the computer course than the art course?

5. In a class of 22 boys and 20 girls, 8 boys wear glasses and 15 girls **do not** wear glasses.

(a) Copy and complete the following table.

	Number of boys	Number of girls	Total number
Wearing glasses	8	⬜	⬜
Not wearing glasses	⬜	15	⬜
Total number =	22	20	42

(b) How many students wear glasses?

(c) How many students **do not** wear glasses?

143

Exercise 2, pages 167-171

6. Devi took a survey of all the families living in her housing development to find the number of children in each family. As she asked each family for the number of children, she wrote the results in a chart. Then she tallied her results.

0	2	1	2	3	2
3	3	2	1	2	2
2	1	0	1	4	5
7	3	2	2	1	1
2	2	3	3	2	4
1	5	1	2	5	2

(a) Complete the tally chart.

Number of children in the family	Number of families	Total number of families
0	//	
1	++++ ///	
2	++++ ++++ ////	
3	++++ /	
4	//	
5	///	
6		
7	/	

(b) How many families did Devi survey?

7. Devi then made a **line plot** of the data.

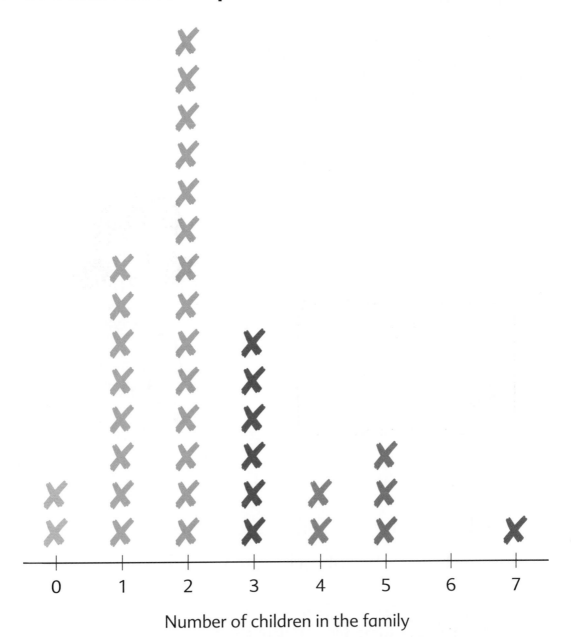

Number of children in the family

(a) What is the number of children found most often?
How many families had this number of children?

(b) The fewest number of families had 6 children.
How many families had 6 children?

(c) What is the difference between the number of families that
had 2 children and the number that had 7 children?

Exercise 3, pages 172-173

② Probability

There are red and green marbles in a bag.
Maria will pick one marble without looking.
What color will she probably pick?

I wonder if there are more red marbles or green marbles...

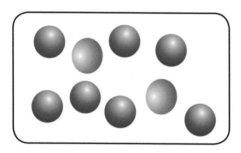

It is **likely** that Maria will pick a red marble.

It is **unlikely** that she will pick a green marble.

An **event** is something that happens.
A **likely** event is one that has a good chance of happening.
An **unlikely** event does not have a good chance of happening.

1. Sammy picks one marble from the bag without looking.

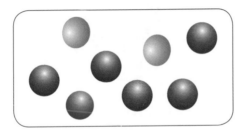

(a) Which color will he most likely get?
(b) Which color will he least likely get?

2. Cindy takes one marble from the bag without looking.

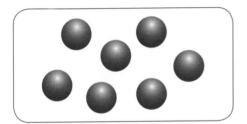

Some events are **certain**. An event is certain if it will always happen.
Some events are **impossible**. An event is impossible if it will never happen.

(a) What color do you think she will get?
(b) Can Cindy get a red marble?
(c) Is it certain or impossible that Cindy will get a blue marble?

3. Anna rolls a regular six-sided die.

Is it certain, likely, unlikely, or impossible that she will get
(a) a number that is greater than 5?
(b) a number that is less than 5?
(c) a 1-digit number?
(d) a number that is greater than 6?

Exercise 4, pages 174-175

4.

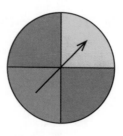

Miguel spins a spinner 20 times and records the results in a tally chart.

Red	Yellow	Blue	Green
~~IIII~~ I	~~IIII~~	IIII	~~IIII~~

(a) The spinner landed on red [ ] times.

(b) The spinner landed on yellow [ ] times.

(c) The spinner landed on blue [ ] times.

(d) The spinner landed on green [ ] times.

5. This bar graph shows the same data.

We can show data from probability experiments in tables and graphs.

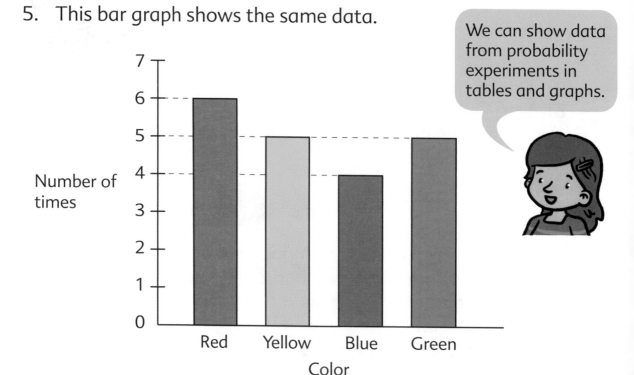

(a) On which color did the spinner land the greatest number of times?
(b) On which color did the spinner land the fewest number of times?
(c) On which colors did the spinner land the same number of times?
(d) How many more times did the spinner land on red than on yellow?
(e) How many fewer times did the spinner land on blue than on red?

6. This bar graph shows the number of times Sally got heads and tails when she flipped a coin many times.

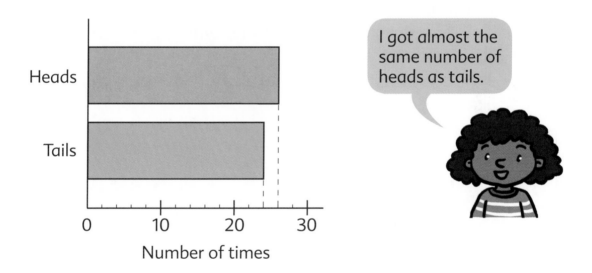

I got almost the same number of heads as tails.

(a) How many times did Sally flip the coin?
(b) Did Sally get more heads or tails?
(c) How many times did she get heads?
(d) How many times did she get tails?
(e) How many more times did she get heads than tails?

Exercise 5, pages 176-177

7. Adam picked a marble from a bag 100 times without looking. He replaced the marble each time.
He put the results in a table.

Color	Number of times
Red	32
Blue	59
Green	9

We can use the data from experiments to make predictions!

(a) What different colors are in the bag?
(b) Which color did Adam pick the most?
(c) Which color did Adam pick the least?
(d) If Adam picks another marble, which color will he most likely get?
(e) If Adam picks another marble, which color will he least likely get?

Exercise 6, pages 178-179

REVIEW 5

Find the value of each of the following. Use estimation to see if your answers are reasonable.

	(a)	(b)	(c)
1.	609 + 92	982 + 128	4976 + 24
2.	820 − 118	903 − 294	3005 − 2096
3.	49 × 6	204 × 7	382 × 9
4.	96 ÷ 6	104 ÷ 7	260 ÷ 8

5. Write **+**, **−**, **×**, or **÷** in place of each ⬤.

   (a) 54 ⬤ 6 = 9   (b) 480 ⬤ 30 = 510

   (c) 50 ⬤ 2 = 10 × 10   (d) 9 ⬤ 8 × 3 = 3 ⬤ 9 × 8

   (e) 60 ⬤ 0 = 60   (f) 60 ⬤ 0 = 0

6. The table shows the number of people who attended four courses in a community center.
   Draw a bar graph to show the data given in the table.

Course	Number of people
Cooking	27
Art	25
Computer	49
Dancing	30

7. Make a table to show the following data.

Kevin
Height: 154 cm
Weight: 41 kg
Age: 11 yr 2 mth

Travis
Height: 153 cm
Weight: 44 kg
Age: 11 yr 10 mth

Seth
Height: 160 cm
Weight: 48 kg
Age: 13 yr 8 mth

8. Look at the bag of marbles on the right.
   Tell whether it is likely, unlikely, certain,
   or impossible to pick each of the following
   from the bag without looking.
   (a) a marble
   (b) a yellow marble
   (c) a green marble
   (d) a white marble

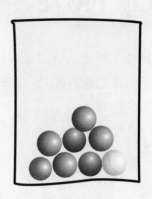

9. Andrea worked in a factory for 9 days.
   She was paid $45 each day.
   How much did she earn altogether?

10. Mrs. Mills paid $56 for 4 dresses.
    Each dress costs the same amount.
    How much did each dress cost?

11. Lily weighs 29 kg.
    Her father is 3 times as heavy as she.
    How much heavier is Lily's father than Lily?

12. Mitch bought 2500 tiles.
    He used 1164 tiles for one room and 940 tiles
    for another room.
    How many tiles were left?

13. 4 people bought a birthday present for their friend.
    They paid the cashier $100 and received $48 change.
    If they shared the cost equally, how much did each
    person pay?

14. Mrs. Barret bought 8 packets of cookies for a party.
    There were 12 cookies in each packet.
    After the party, there were 28 cookies left.
    How many cookies were eaten at the party?

Review 5, pages 180-184

GLOSSARY

Word	Meaning
certain	An event is **certain** if it will always happen. If you roll a regular 6-sided die, it is **certain** that you will get a number that is from 1 to 6.
difference	To find the **difference** between two numbers, we subtract the smaller number from the greater number. $$142 - 21 = 121$$ The **difference** between 142 and 21 is 121.
estimation	When we **estimate** an answer, we round the parts of the question so that we can find an answer quickly. This gives us an answer that is about the same as the actual answer. $312 + 48$ is about $300 + 50$. Thus, the value of $312 + 48$ is about $$300 + 50 = 350$$

Word	Meaning
even numbers	Numbers in which the ones digit is 0, 2, 4, 6 or 8 are called **even numbers**.
event	An **event** is something that happens. Every time you roll a die to get a number, that is an **event**.
expanded form	We write the **expanded form** of the number 4198 like this: $$4000 + 100 + 90 + 8$$
impossible	An event is **impossible** if it will never happen. If you roll a regular 6-sided die, it is **impossible** to get a number that is greater than 6.
likely	A **likely** event is one that has a good chance of happening. If you roll a regular 6-sided die, it is **likely** that you will get a number that is less than 5.

Word	Meaning
line plot	A **line plot** is a graph that shows how often an event happens.

Word	Meaning
odd numbers	Numbers in which the ones digit is 1, 3, 5, 7 or 9 are called **odd numbers**.
place	

Thousands	Hundreds	Tens	Ones
2	1	8	3

In **2**183, the digit **2** is the thousands **place**.

Word	Meaning
product	To find the **product** of two numbers, we multiply the numbers.

$$42 \times 6 = 252$$

The **product** of 42 and 6 is 252.

Word	Meaning
quotient	When we divide one number by another, the answer we get is called the **quotient**. $$15 \div 3 = 5$$ The **quotient** is 5.
remainder	When we divide one number by another, the number that is left over is called the **remainder**. $$16 \div 3 = 5 \text{ R } 1$$ The quotient is 5. The **remainder** is 1. We write it as $16 \div 3 = 5$ **R** 1.
rounding	When we **round** a number, we change the number to the nearest ten, nearest hundred or nearest thousand. 12 rounded to the nearest ten is 10. 17 rounded to the nearest ten is 20.

Word	Meaning
standard form	7639 is how we write the **standard form** of the number seven thousand, six hundred thirty-nine.
sum	To find the **sum** of two numbers, we add the numbers together. $$142 + 21 = 163$$ The **sum** of 142 and 21 is 163.
unlikely	An **unlikely** event does not have a good chance of happening. If you roll a regular 6-sided die, it is **unlikely** that you will get a number that is greater than 5.
value	The **value** of a digit in a number is the amount the digit represents in the number. In 2**7**14, the **value** of the digit **7** is 700.

Index

Blank

Blank